Martin Luther KING, Jr.

*Spirit-Led
Prophet*

Richard Deats

MARTIN LUTHER
KING, JR.

Spirit-Led
Prophet

A Biography

Foreword by
Coretta Scott King

New City Press
London   New York   Manila

Published in the United States by New City Press
202 Cardinal Rd., Hyde Park, NY 12538
www.newcitypress.com
©2000 Richard Deats.

Cover design by Nick Cianfarani

Library of Congress Cataloging-in-Publication Data:

Deats, Richard L., 1932-
   Martin Luther King, Jr., spirit-led prophet : a biography / Richard Deats ; foreword by
Coretta Scott King.
     p. cm.
  ISBN 1-56548-097-X
   1. King, Martin Luther, Jr., 1929-1968. 2. King, Martin Luther, Jr.,
1929-1968--Religion. 3. King, Martin Luther, Jr., 1929-1968--Ethics. 4.
Afro-Americans--Biography. 5. Civil rights workers--United States--Biography. 6.
Baptists--United States--Clergy--Biography. 7. Nonviolence--Religious
aspects--Christianity. I. Title.

  E185.97.K5 D42 1999
  323'.092--dc21
  [B]

                                     99-051952

Scripture quotations are from the Revised Standard Version © 1973.

Printed in Canada

To

My Haitian-American grandchildren:
Lin, Christina and Jimmy

And my Israeli-American grandchildren:
Rafael, Danya, Tova, Nechoma,
Moishe, Joseph, Aaron, Rifka, and David

With the prayer that they may,
in their own way,
help fulfill Martin Luther King's vision
of the Beloved Community

Contents

Foreword

Some of the biographies written about my husband, Martin Luther King, Jr., thus far have done a good job of explaining the events of his life and leadership. But I have long felt that few of them did an adequate job of illuminating his moral and spiritual beliefs as a God-centered man.

Martin was a third-generation Christian minister, and this was the moral and spiritual foundation and vital center of the faith that empowered his leadership. As he wrote in his first book, *Stride Toward Freedom*, of the technique of nonviolent resistance first employed in the Montgomery Bus Boycott, "Christ furnished the spirit and motivation, while Gandhi furnished the method."

When asked for references that address his moral and spiritual perspectives, I have recommended my husband's books, *Strength to Love, The Measure of A Man* and *A Knock at Midnight* as the best guides to his faith and philosophy. Martin wrote six books (not including posthumous collections of his speeches and sermons) and dozens of articles, as well as delivering hundreds of speeches and sermons. Thus, there has been a need for a long-time for a concise, updated guide focused on his spiritual life.

In *Martin Luther King, Jr.: Spirit-Led Prophet*, author Richard Deats has made a significant contribution to meeting this need. He discusses with unique insight some of my husband's most revealing, yet overlooked writings about his most deeply-felt values, shedding new light on his religious and philosophical views. Rev. Deats, editor of *Fellowship* magazine and a veteran organizer for the Fellowship of Reconciliation, is one of America's most knowledgeable and dedicated advocates of nonviolence. He brings a perspective heretofore missing from books about my husband—that of an activist who has not only written about nonviolence, but who has "walked the walk" in numerous nonviolent action campaigns.

Martin Luther King, Jr., pastor, theologian, activist leader and ardent advocate of nonviolent social change, was fundamentally a moral and spiritual leader. In these pages, readers will find a fresh perspective on his meditations on spiritual concerns, such as the power of prayer, unearned suffering for a just cause, forgiveness, love of enemies and the moral obligation to confront and challenge injustice. They show how Martin integrated what he called "the love ethic" into every aspect of his life, as well as the nonviolent movements he led.

Richard Deats considers the influence of a range of theologians, philosophers and writers and their ideas on my husband's spiritual development. He shows how Martin synthesized their wisdom with his perspective as a committed Christian minister to pose a powerful moral challenge to racial injustice, poverty and militarism. These beliefs are the well-springs which nourished and empowered the nonviolent revolution that would change America and inspire liberation movements all over the world.

Richard Deats has produced in this work an invaluable spiritual portrait of Martin Luther King, Jr. and the sources of his faith, courage and willingness to offer his life to the nonviolent struggle against violence, racial and economic injustice. These teachings, so well-revealed in this unique biography, have endured because they continue to offer hope and inspiration for all who would fulfill the Dream.

Coretta Scott King

Introduction

In the winter of 1958 I was part of an inter-racial group of graduate students at Boston University School of Theology that drove home for the Christmas holidays. We were all from the South, each of us a part of the civil rights movement, each of us proud to be students at the school from which Martin Luther King, Jr. had graduated a few years earlier. I had written to Dr. King and told him that we would be worshiping in his congregation at Dexter Avenue Baptist Church on our way through Montgomery. 1958 was after the Montgomery Bus Boycott but still prior to the Freedom Rides of the 1960s. An inter-racial group driving through the South in those days was still uncommon and a bit risky. The day before we reached Montgomery we paid a visit to Koinonia Farm near Americus, Georgia, a pioneering inter-racial experiment in the heart of the South. Clarence Jordan, biblical scholar and one of Koinonia's founders, told us of the harassment and danger they lived under. Their fruit trees had been cut down, their farm stand by the highway dynamited, their houses shot up. They had been expelled from the local Baptist Church, accused of be-

reeted. At the end of the service we planned to head for
meet us, after which they both invited us to have Sunday
King family. Busy schedules and the demands of giving

Those memories have stayed with me in the subsequent
years as Martin Luther King's life and witness have had a
continuing impact on our world.

Assassinated in 1968 at the young age of thirty-nine,
King's twelve-year ministry burned into humanity's con-
sciousness like a comet streaking across a starless night.
Similar to Mahatma Gandhi, Martin Luther King, Jr. led a
freedom movement of the oppressed through the way of
nonviolence, spiritually grounded and firm in its renuncia-
tion of violence but radical in its pursuit of justice. To an
age reeling from the relentless spread of weapons of mass
destruction coupled with violence and injustice at home,
King held out a hopeful and bold alternative to violent
coannihilation: overcome evil with good, make friends of

enemies, pursue justice through nonviolence, build the Beloved Community. In the years since King's death, individuals and groups have been experimenting with nonviolent ways to bring freedom, justice, and peace to this planet and, in the words of King's last book, move "from chaos to community."

King's fame grows year by year. In 1979, on the occasion of the fiftieth year of King's birth, President Jimmy Carter, in a service at Ebenezer Baptist Church, called for a national holiday to mark his birthday. In 1983, Dr. King's birth date was proclaimed a national holiday in a bill signed by President Reagan in the Rose Garden at the White House, with members of Congress and civil rights leaders gathered for the occasion. I was there that day as a member of the Martin Luther King Federal Holiday Commission, which was established to foster the national observance of King's birthday. These observances are held today not only all over the United States but throughout the world as well. Boulevards, community centers, parks, buildings and monuments have been named in his honor. The implications of his life and teaching are being studied in seminaries and universities.

Yet, ironically, as the era of King's life recedes into the background, many who honor King as a national hero overly emphasize the spellbinding orator who delivered the "I Have a Dream" speech at the Lincoln Monument. The Dreamer is honored; why he was killed is glossed over. The burning prophetic fire in him that illumined the dark recesses of our national life—what he called the triple evils of racism, materialism, and militarism—is still too intense for our timid hearts. And, in the final analysis, his nonviolence creed is rejected in both the domestic and foreign policies of the United States.

What manner of man was the Rev. Martin Luther King, Jr. — pastor, theologian, scholar, orator, civil rights leader, martyr? The focus of this book will be to examine the life and thought of Dr. King, particularly those beliefs that shaped who he was, that sustained him, that gave his life meaning, and that moved this spirit-led prophet to discover and fulfill his destiny, whatever the cost.

The Call to and Preparation for Ministry

Martin Luther King, Jr., was born on January 15, 1929 at 501 Auburn Avenue in Atlanta, Georgia, the son of Martin Luther King, Sr., and Alberta Christine Williams King. He was the second child of the family, having one brother and one sister. He descended from families deeply shaped by their Baptist faith; the stamp of the Southern black church was unmistakable in the King and Williams families. Fervent preaching and powerful gospel singing provided the church community with a strong source of faith seen in the prayer meetings, the revivals, the community dinners, and the social witness. Martin Luther King, Sr.—"Daddy" King as he was affectionately called — was a well-known pastor and community leader, who courageously supported the welfare of the black community and forthrightly opposed segregation whenever he encountered it. Alberta Williams was the daughter of renown pastor and preacher A. D. Williams, who was minister of Atlanta's prestigious

Ebenezer Baptist Church from 1894 until his death in 1931, at which time King, Sr., succeeded his father-in-law as the minister of Ebenezer.[1]

Young Martin grew up in the fairly secure and established life of Atlanta's black middle-class community. His parents and his grandparents provided strong role models for the sensitive Martin. He was particularly influenced by his saintly grandmother, Jennie Celeste Williams. Even in this rather privileged family life, where love was central, he experienced the bitter and unjust impact of segregation that was the lot of all Southern blacks. The legacy of slavery was still harshly present in the attitudes held and laws enforced throughout the South.

Martin had a white childhood playmate, but when they began school they went to separate, segregated schools, and their friendship ended when the white boy's father told him he couldn't play with Martin anymore. This led Martin's parents to discuss with him for the first time the race problem and the suffering black people endured because of it. As a teenager, Martin felt humiliated by the segregated — and unequal — schools, movie theaters, waiting rooms, toilets, etc.

Tempted to hate the perpetrators of such cruelty, young Martin was admonished by his parents to "never stoop so low as to let anybody make you hate," as Daddy King would often say to his family and his congregation. And Martin's mother, as well as his father, told him that the Christian was to respond with love to his oppressors. This did not mean submitting to oppression: Young Martin often saw his father, at considerable risk, speak out against segregation and refuse to abide by the pernicious Jim Crow laws that governed race relations in the South. King, Sr. refused to ride the city's segregated buses and led the fight to

---

1. Carson, *Papers of Martin Luther King, Jr.* I:18-28.

eliminate segregated elevators in the courthouse. Both Daddy King and grandfather A. D. Williams courageously fought for justice and served as powerful role models to the impressionable Martin, Jr. His strong mother was an equally important role model, telling her son when he first faced the harsh reality of racism, "You must never feel that you are less than somebody else. You must always feel that you are somebody."[2] Nonetheless, it took Martin years to overcome his antipathy to white people.

Martin was very precocious; he had a critical, inquisitive mind. As early as in his twelfth year of age, he began to raise questions about the literalistic interpretation of the Bible. Too many questions were left unanswered, too many issues unresolved. An excellent student, Martin was admitted to Atlanta's Morehouse College as an early admissions freshman in 1944—when he was only fifteen! At first he thought of becoming a lawyer, expressing distaste for the fundamentalism and emotionalism of many of the Southern black churches, as well as for their lack of engagement in dealing with the ills of society, focusing rather on "the sweet by and by." But at Morehouse, the great Benjamin Mays, president of the college, and King's religion professor George Kelsey helped Martin Jr. catch a vision of the high calling of the ministry that included critical thinking and social witness. President Mays, who had visited India in 1936, often mentioned Gandhi and India's freedom struggle in his lectures. While at Morehouse, King read Henry David Thoreau's "On Civil Disobedience," which taught that one should refuse to cooperate with an evil system. This revolutionary idea began to germinate in the fertile mind and searching spirit of the young scholar.[3] Eventually he decided to dedicate his life to God and the Christian ministry. Before he graduated, he was ordained and in 1947 became the

---

2. Carson, *Papers of Martin Luther King, Jr.* I:33-35.
3. King, Jr., *Stride Toward Freedom,* 91.

associate pastor of Ebenezer Baptist Church, where his father was the head minister.[4]

It was not until seminary, however, that King began to fully develop his intellectual abilities. In 1948 he entered Crozer Theological Seminary in Chester, Pennsylvania. Only nineteen, he was younger than his classmates and was one of only eleven black seminarians among a student body of almost one hundred. At this Baptist institution, he was particularly influenced by professors indebted to the writings of Walter Rauschenbusch, the leading theologian of the social gospel. Rauschenbusch's thought helped King develop a theological framework in which the Gospel is understood as addressing not only individuals but the whole of society in both a spiritual and material sense. The thought of Reinhold Niebuhr persuaded King of the stubborn persistence of evil and the inadequacy of liberal optimism in dealing with the ills of society. George Hegel's understanding of dialectic — that every situation brings about a reaction out of which a new situation is created — profoundly helped King understand social change. He was deeply moved by a lecture on pacifism by A .J. Muste of the Fellowship of Reconciliation, although he was not at that time convinced of its practicability. However, a sermon on Mahatma Gandhi by Mordecai Johnson, president of Howard University, had such an impact on King — he called it "profound and electrifying" — that he went out from the meeting and immediately bought half a dozen books on Gandhi. In them he discovered what he had been searching for—a way for Christians to address not just personal evils (like lying and stealing) but also social evils (such as racism and war), taking seriously sin and evil without abandoning Jesus' teaching about the centrality of love in the life of faith. King had long been struggling with the

---

4. Carson, *Papers of Martin Luther King, Jr.* I:37-45; cf. King, Jr., *Stride Toward Freedom,* 91.

evil of both race prejudice and economic injustice. He judged both capitalism and communism as partial and grossly inadequate economic systems. In Gandhi he found the method to apply the love ethic of Jesus for resisting evil and changing society. This was not *passive nonresistance* but *nonviolent resistance* to evil that could be "a social force on a large scale."[5] This discovery of Gandhi became a major event in King's spiritual journey.

At Crozer, King not only excelled in his studies. He was president and valedictorian of his class, named "most outstanding student" and received a scholarship for graduate study. Influenced by the personalist theology of Edgar S. Brightman while at Crozer, King applied and was accepted for doctoral study at Boston University School of Theology where Brightman taught. Personalism helped King appropriate the importance of religious experience in understanding God as personal, and it convinced him that personality, both human and divine, was where one found the meaning of ultimate reality. King wrote his dissertation in the field of systematic theology, working under the able teaching of Brightman and L. Harold deWolf. His dissertation was entitled, "A Comparison of the Conceptions of God in the Thinking of Paul Tillich and Henry Nelson Weiman." He was very appreciative of certain aspects of the thought of both Tillich and Weiman. But in the end he rejected their denial of the personality of God and affirmed his belief in a personal God in whom, as King wrote, "there is feeling and will, responsive to the deepest yearnings of the human heart; this God both evokes and answers prayer."[6]

Graduate study at Boston University School of Theology, the oldest Methodist seminary in the United States, also brought him into contact with many exponents of

---

5. Carson, *Papers of Martin Luther King, Jr.* I:45-57; King, Jr., *Stride Toward Freedom*, 94-99.
6. Carson, *Papers of Martin Luther King, Jr.* II:1-4.

pacifism, nonviolence, and the social gospel, such as Dean Walter Muelder, Allan Knight Chalmers, S. Paul Schilling, and Howard Thurman, Dean of the University Chapel and African-American preacher, mystic, and writer. Thurman, who was a classmate of Martin's father at Morehouse College and was a close family friend, came to Boston University during Martin's last year there and became a life-long friend and mentor.[7]

King frequently had opportunities to preach, and he became well known as a very powerful preacher. He returned to Atlanta whenever possible, keeping strong the ties to his family and to the church there. He had close friendships with black students on the campus, and he was part of a group called the Dialectical Society, which met monthly to read papers and discuss theological issues particularly as they related to the African-American community.

While he was in Boston he met Coretta Scott of Alabama, who was a student at the New England Conservatory of Music. Their courtship led to their marriage on June 18, 1953. They were married at the Scott's home in rural Alabama, where King, Sr. performed the service. Unable to stay at the segregated hotels in the area, the couple spent the first night of their marriage at the home of some friends. In 1954, having completed the course work for his degree, King accepted the call to become pastor of Dexter Avenue Baptist Church in Montgomery, Alabama. He chose to return to the South, even though he was offered significant church and academic positions in various parts of the country. After the couple went to Montgomery, he completed

---

7. Howard Thurman, *With Head and Heart* (New York: Harcourt, Brace, Jovanovich, 1979), 254f. I entered the doctoral program at Boston University in 1957 and had the opportunity to study under these same scholars and hear them speak of King's years at the seminary.

his doctoral dissertation and was awarded his Ph.D. on June 5, 1955.[8]

Throughout his seminary and graduate study in northern seminaries with predominantly European-American faculties and student bodies, King's experience, thought and faith broadened and deepened profoundly. Yet he remained unmistakenly rooted and grounded in the tradition of the black church from which he came.

8. Carson, *Papers of Martin Luther King, Jr.* II:5-47.

Son of the Black Church

The faith of Martin Luther King, Jr. was nurtured in the black Baptist tradition of the South. King, the theologian and scholar of personalism, the prophet of the social gospel and of nonviolence, never lost his roots in the black church. His maternal great-grandfather and grandfather, and his father were all black Baptist preachers of a religious tradition that grew out of the days of slavery of African forbears, who had been brought to these shores against their will and who, even after their manumission, suffered continuing racist violence and second-class citizenship.

The black religious tradition was a faith that sustained and embolded its adherents in the face of adversity. The black Baptist tradition was full of fire and passion. Its preachers proclaimed their faith through emotional sermons that evoked verbal responses, clapping, tears, and laughter from the worshipers. Long Bible passages were recited from memory, and Bible stories were told with imagination and originality. Choirs led the congregations in fervent singing of hymns and spirituals. The music brought solace — "Nobody knows the trouble I've seen, Nobody knows but Jesus." "There is a balm in Gilead to make the wounded whole. There is a balm in Gilead to heal the sin-sick soul."

They also sang of a prophetic faith calling for freedom— "Go down Moses, Go down to Egyptland, Go tell ol' Pharaoh, Let my people go!" The old gospel song of slave days, "Hold On" still spoke to a people in bondage:

> Paul and Silas bound in jail
> Had nobody for to go their bail
> Keep your hand on that plow,
> Hold on, Hold on
>
> Paul and Silas began to shout
> Jail door opened and they walked out
> Keep your hand on that plow,
> Hold on, Hold on
>
> God gave Noah the rainbow sign
> No more water, the fire next time
> Keep your hand on that plow,
> Hold on, Hold on
>
> The only chain a man can stand
> Is the chain from hand to hand
> Keep your hand on that plow
> Hold on

Verses were added, words changed, as the songs of liberation were taken on the marches and demonstrations. Thus to "Hold On" were added such verses as:

> Got my hand on the freedom plow
> Wouldn't take nothing for my journey now
> Keep your eyes on the prize
> Hold on, Hold on.

The only thing that we did wrong
Stayed in the wilderness a day too long
Keep your eyes on the prize
Hold on, Hold on.

The only time that we did right
Was the day we began our fight
Keep your eyes on the prize
Hold on.[1]

This is not to imply that most, even many, in the black church supported Dr. King and the others who directly challenged the segregated status quo in the South. The prophetic tradition has always faced great resistance, not only in society at large, but in the community of faith. The biblical prophets were usually rejected, persecuted, stoned, driven out. Jesus reminded those who would follow his way, "Blessed are you when men shall revile you, and persecute you, and utter all kinds of evil against you falsely on my account" (Mt5:11). It is not surprising then that many feared the upsetting of the established order. It could bring loss of jobs and friends, as well as unleashing racist violence and vicious reprisals. It was a new and uncharted journey striking off into freedom land, and many were accustomed to an otherworldly Gospel that prepared people for the next world, not for challenging the injustices of this one.

When King and the other new visionaries tried to get their powerful church, the five million strong National Baptist Convention, to march to the drumbeat of freedom, the established leadership — under the direction of the Rev. Joseph H. Jackson — soundly rejected their call, leading eventually to a rupture in the church. The Jackson forces beat back the political threat to their leadership, even going

---

1. Words provided by Dorothy Cotton in a letter to the author.

to the extent of having Martin Luther King excommuni-
cated. This resulted in a split in the denomination with
many progressive pastors, including Dr. King and the President of Morehouse College, Dr. Benjamin Mays, walking
out to form the Progressive Baptist Church. The enmity of
the old guard leadership continued long after King's assassination. A vivid illustration of this occurred when Chicago
renamed South Parkway Dr. Martin Luther King, Jr. Drive.
Joseph Jackson's mammoth Olivet Baptist Church was
located on South Parkway. So that the address of his
church would not have to bear the name of King, Jackson
got his church to spend fifty thousand dollars to close up
the South Parkway entrance and build a new entrance on
the side street![2]

Another example of resistance to the leadership of King
and the Southern Christian Leadership Council (SCLC)
occurred in Birmingham. When the decision was made to
come to Birmingham in the spring of 1963, the black Baptist
clergy of Birmingham as a group voted to oppose Dr. King's
coming there. Of the four hundred black Baptist churches
in Birmingham, only fourteen agreed to open their doors to
mass meetings for the campaign.[3]

Nonetheless, such opposition did not deter the movement from its calling. Dr. King was a spirit-led prophet
awakening the wider church to this new vision and respon-
sibilities. And even as the religious establishment opposed
the movement, King continued to draw on the strength of
that heritage, taking from the altar the fire, not the ashes.
We see this clearly in his sermons, which resonate with the
cadence and style of the black church. He was an intellectual who never lost his common touch. He could appeal to a
rural congregation in the South as well as to a civil rights
rally in the North. His sermons and speeches evidenced

2. Miller, *Martin Luther King, Jr.*, 96, 125. Branch, *Pillar of Fire*, 25-29.
3. Young, *An Easy Burden*, 209.

serious biblical and historical scholarship, yet were delivered with an emotional power that seldom failed to deeply
move those who heard them. He often evoked biblical
images and quoted from hymns and spirituals, especially as
he moved to the climax of his presentations. A typical example is seen in his sermon "The Drum Major Instinct," where
he repeats the phrase "Every now and then" and "I want
you to say" as he moves powerfully to the climax of his
address:

> Every now and then I guess we all think realisti-
> cally about the days when we will be victimized
> with what is life's final common denomina-
> tor—that something we call death. We all think
> about it. And every now and then I think about
> my own death, and I think about my own funeral.
> And I don't think of it in a morbid sense. Every
> now and then I ask myself, "What is it that I
> would want said?" And I leave the word to you
> this morning.
>
> If any of you are around when I have to meet
> my day, I don't want a long funeral. And if you get
> somebody to deliver the eulogy, tell them not to
> talk too long. Every now and then I wonder what I
> want them to say. Tell them not to mention that I
> have a Nobel Peace Prize, that isn't important.
> Tell them not to mention that I have three or four
> hundred other awards, that's not important. Tell
> him not to mention where I went to school.
>
> I'd like somebody to mention that day, that
> Martin Luther King, Jr. tried to give his life serv-
> ing others. I'd like somebody to say that day, that
> Martin Luther King, Jr. tried to love somebody. I
> want you to say that day, that I tried to be right
> on the war question. I want you to be able to say

that day, that I did try to feed the hungry. And I want you to be able to say that day, that I did try, in my life, to clothe those who were naked. I want you to say that day, that I did try, in my life, to visit those who were in prison. I want you to say that I tried to love and serve humanity.

Yes, if you want to say that I was a drum major, say that I was a drum major for justice; say that I was drum major for peace; I was a drum major for righteousness. And all of the other shallow things will not matter. I won't have any money to leave behind. I won't have the fine and luxurious things of life to leave behind. But I just want to leave a committed life behind.

And that's all I want to say . . . if I can help somebody as I pass along, if I can cheer somebody with a word or song, if I can show somebody he's traveling wrong, then my living will not be in vain. If I can do my duty as a Christian ought, if I can bring salvation to a world once wrought, if I can spread the message as the master taught, then my living will not be in vain.

Yes Jesus, I want to be on your right or your left side, not for any selfish reason. I want to be on your right or your best side, not in terms of some political kingdom or ambition, but I just want to be there in love and in justice and in truth and in commitment to others, so that we can make of this old world a new world.[4]

---

4. Washington, "The drum major instinct" in *Testament of Hope,* 266-267.

The Providential Choice
of Montgomery

But we have gotten ahead of our story. After graduating from Boston University School of Theology, Martin Luther King, Jr. accepted the pulpit of the historic Dexter Avenue Baptist Church in Montgomery, Alabama. Looking back, the move to Montgomery seems providential, part of a wider divine plan, as King was later to write when he reflected on all that happened as a result of the Montgomery bus boycott:

> Whatever the name, some extra-human force labors to create a harmony out of the discords of the universe. There is a creative power that works to pull down mountains of evil and level hilltops of injustice. God still works through history His wonders to perform. It seems as though God had decided to use Montgomery as the proving ground for the struggle and triumph of freedom and justice in America. And what better place for

it than the leading symbol of the Old South! It is
one of the splendid ironies of our day that Montgomery, the Cradle of the Confederacy, is being
transformed into Montgomery, the cradle of freedom and justice.[1]

King came to Montgomery at a time when momentous
stirrings were taking place in the country. On May 17, 1954
the U. S. Supreme Court, in *Brown vs. Board of Education of
Topeka,* declared "separate but equal" public schools as
unconstitutional. The Southern way of life was being fundamentally challenged. Dr. King saw his calling as not only
serving the Dexter Avenue congregation but the wider community as well. He became active in the local chapters of
the National Association for the Advancement of Colored
People (NAACP) and the Southern Regional Council and
their efforts against racism.

Like all other Southern cities, Montgomery had segregated city buses in which the white passengers sat at the
front and Negro passengers in the back.[2] On December 1,
1955 Rosa Parks was arrested when she refused to move to
the back of the bus to make room for boarding white passengers. Parks, a seamstress active in the NAACP, had
received nonviolence training in the summer of 1955 at the
pioneer Highlander Folk School in Monteagle, Tennessee.
Highlander, founded in 1932 by Miles Horton, was one of
the early seedbeds of education and training for progressive
social change in the South. Parks knew that what she was
doing was a radical act, a purposeful gauntlet thrown down
to Southern-style racism. The Women's Political Council, a
key organization of Negro women in Montgomery, had
already challenged the city's segregated buses and had

---

1. King, Jr., *Stride Toward Freedom,* 70.
2. Seveny percent of the riders were black. They had to enter the bus by the front door, pay
   the fare, then exit and enter by the back door.

threatened a boycott if changes were not made. When Parks was arrested, the Council's president Jo Ann Gibson Robinson went to work with some students to mimeograph tens of thousands of leaflets calling for a bus boycott. The leaflets were then quietly distributed throughout the black community, followed by a community meeting at which the Montgomery Improvement Association (MIA) was formed. The boycott was endorsed and Dr. King was elected the Association's president. Though only twenty-six years old he was superbly trained, spiritually grounded and gifted in leadership abilities. The ensuing 381-day bus boycott became the laboratory in which King's study of the Gandhian approach to social change was put to the test.[3] It was seven years after Gandhi's assassination (in 1948).

He was later to write that the experience of the long boycott was to teach him more about nonviolence than all the books he had read. "Living through the actual experience of the protest, nonviolence became more than a method to which I gave intellectual assent, it became a commitment to a way of life. Many issues I had not cleared up intellectually concerning nonviolence were now solved in the sphere of political action."[4] Two pacifists deeply experienced in nonviolence, Glenn Smiley—a white Texas Methodist minister from the Fellowship of Reconciliation — and Bayard Rustin, an African-American Quaker with the War Resisters' League—spent a great deal of time with King and the MIA, sharing their long experience and understanding of the theory and practice of nonviolence.

Bayard Rustin, a conscientious objector in World War II, had gone to prison because of his pacifist beliefs. Until

---

3. *Stride Toward Freedom,* King's best-selling and first book, is a detailed, compelling account of the Montgomery bus boycott. The complete account of the Women's Political Council is found in *The Montgomery Bus Boycott and the Women Who Started It: The Memoir of Jo Ann Gibson Robinson,* ed. David J. Garrow (Knoxville: University of Tennessee Press, 1987).
4. King, Jr., *Stride Toward Freedom,* 101.

1953 he had worked for the Fellowship of Reconciliation (FOR) as its race-relations secretary, then as its staff member for college work. He was a participant in the 1947 Journey of Reconciliation, the first freedom ride into the South that challenged interstate segregation. He had also spent six months in India studying Gandhi. A brilliant strategist and organizer, Rustin was to play a crucial role in the movement in the years to come. In Montgomery he in effect became King's secretary and served as a seasoned adviser in the boycott.

Glenn Smiley was sent to Montgomery to assist the movement in whatever way he could. Like Rustin, he, too, had served in prison as a conscientious objector and was an experienced teacher and practitioner of nonviolence. In Smiley's first meeting with King, a four-fold assignment was laid out for Glenn:

1) Dr. King wanted to learn everything Smiley knew about nonviolence, especially the practical application of it as it had been developing in various projects around the country.

2) Smiley would work with the leadership of the churches and of Montgomery on the subject of nonviolence, particularly with regards to the bus boycott.

3) Smiley, who had been working throughout the South, would help develop a support network and leadership in the black community.

4) Smiley would try to be a bridge to the white churches and the wider community in Montgomery.

Smiley spent the next year working in Montgomery and other places carrying out this assignment. He preached, spoke and did nonviolence training in most of the black churches in Montgomery. He found very little access to the white churches although he did develop friendships with some of the white clergy.[5]

---

5. Glenn Smiley, *Nonviolence. The Gentle Persuader* (Nyack, NY: Fellowship Publications, 1991), 4-5.

On February 28, 1956, Smiley wrote a letter to over two dozen people in the Fellowship of Reconciliation, who were Christians deeply rooted in prayer, such as Muriel Lester, Howard Thurman, Allan Hunter, and Bishop Matthew Clair. Describing the Montgomery boycott, he wrote: "The die has been cast, there is a crisis of terrifying intensity, and I believe that God has called Martin Luther King to lead a great movement here and in the South. But why does God lay such a burden on one so young, so inexperienced, so good? King can be a Negro Gandhi. . . . That is why I am writing [to] more than two dozen people of prayer across the nation, asking that they hold Martin Luther King in the light. Of his own free will, he has sought counsel from some of us older. May he burst like fruit out of season, into the type of leader required for this hour."[6] Certainly the prayers of these and many others helped bring spiritual power to King and the nascent movement.

In February, 1957 the Southern Christian Leadership Council (SCLC) was founded to give direction to the civil rights movement. King was elected its first president. He was under enormous pressure and demands from all sides. He preached, lectured, wrote, and raised money as he was increasingly seen as the major spokesman for the emerging civil rights movement in the country. On the forefront of the challenge to segregation and all forms of racism, King's growing prominence and fame also aroused enormous denunciation and antipathy from those wedded to the status quo.

---

6. Files of the Fellowship of Reconciliation (DG 13, Series E, Box 16, Southern Work Correspondence 1955-1958 of Glenn Smiley, John Swomley and Al Hassler), Swarthmore Peace Collection.

The Kitchen Prayer:
Assurance Out of Anguish

"The dark night of the soul" is a recurring theme in the lives of prophets, saints , and mystics. Commitment to God does not spare one from doubt and anguish in the faith journey. Dr. King's life was no exception.

When the Montgomery bus boycott started, not only King but also his family were subjected to continual vilification and death threats. By the time the boycott was a month old, the Kings were receiving thirty to forty threatening letters and phone calls *each day*. Many were crude and obscene diatribes against blacks and Jews, claiming to be based on the Bible.

In time, the constant threats began to take a severe toll, especially after a white friend told King that he was hearing plans of King's assassination. Others spoke of similar plots and warned King of the dangers facing him. It became harder and harder not to be fearful. As King would later recount:

> One night toward the end of January I settled into bed late, after a strenuous day. Coretta had

already fallen asleep and just as I was about to doze off the telephone rang. An angry voice said, "Listen, nigger, we've taken all we want from you; before next week you'll be sorry you ever came to Montgomery." I hung up, but I couldn't sleep. It seemed that all of my fears had come down on me at once. I had reached the saturation point.

I got out of bed and began to walk the floor. Finally I went to the kitchen and heated a pot of coffee. I was ready to give up. With my cup of coffee sitting untouched before me I tried to think of a way to move out of the picture without appearing a coward. In this state of exhaustion, when my courage had all but gone, I decided to take my problem to God. With my head in my hands, I bowed over the kitchen table and prayed aloud. The words I spoke to God that midnight are still vivid in my memory.

"I am here taking a stand for what I believe is right. But now I am afraid. The people are looking to me for leadership, and if I stand before them without strength and courage, they too will falter. I am at the end of my powers. I have nothing left. I've come to the point where I can't face it alone."

At that moment I experienced the presence of the Divine as I had never experienced Him before. It seemed as though I could hear the quiet assurance of an inner voice saying: "Stand up for righteousness, stand up for truth; and God will be at your side forever." Almost at once my fears began to go. My uncertainty disappeared. I was ready to face anything.[1]

---

1. King, Jr., *Stride Toward Freedom*, 132-138.

Three nights later, on January 30, that resolve was tested when his home was bombed. Rushing home from a mass meeting at the First Baptist Church, King was relieved to find that Coretta and their baby, Yoki, were unharmed, although the house was badly damaged. The mayor and a number of reporters had already arrived. An angry crowd of up to a thousand had gathered in front of the King parsonage, ready to retaliate. King, steadied by his deep experience of the "kitchen prayer," told the crowd not to return evil for evil but to meet hate with love. He said, "We must love our white brothers no matter what they do to us. We must make them know that we love them. Jesus still cries out in words that echo across the centuries: 'Love your enemies; bless them that curse you, pray for them that despitefully use you.' This is what we must live by. We must meet hate with love. Remember, if I am stopped, this movement will not stop, because God is with the movement. Go home with this glowing faith and this radiant assurance."[2]

As would happen so many times, King's words that night calmed the crowd, averting further violence.

In the aftermath of the bombing, officials of the Dexter Avenue Church and other friends urged King to get armed protection. He eventually agreed and went to the sheriff's office to get a permit to carry a gun in his car.

In discussions with Coretta, however, he saw the inconsistency of having a gun and armed bodyguards while believing in and preaching nonviolence. This inner struggle recalls the time when William Penn, young in the faith, asked George Fox, founder of the Quakers, if he could continue to carry a sword. "Carry it as long as thou canst," replied Fox.[3] Like Penn, King was disarmed by his faith as he came to the realization that he could not carry a gun nor

---

2. King, Jr., *Stride Toward Freedom*, 137.
3. Or, as Glenn Smiley said to King, "When the gun gets too heavy, you will lay it down."

be protected by armed men any longer. Step by step, his commitment to nonviolence deepened and intensified.[4]

At another time of discouragement during the Montgomery boycott, King was deeply influenced by the simple faith of a poor, uneducated, elderly woman called "Mother Pollard." After weeks of the boycott had passed, she is remembered for saying, "My feets is tired, but my soul is rested." She was an exemplar of what Gandhi was referring to when he said, "Strength does not come from physical capacity, it comes from an indomitable will."

During one particularly difficult time, Mother Pollard was especially perceptive of the toll that events were taking on King. As he recounts it,

> At the end of the meeting, Mother Pollard came to the front of the church and said, "Come here, son." I immediately went to her and hugged her affectionately. "Something is wrong with you," she said. "You didn't talk strong tonight." Seeking further to disguise my fears, I retorted, "Oh, no, Mother Pollard, nothing is wrong. I am feeling as fine as ever." But her insight was discerning. "Now you can't fool me," she said. "I knows something is wrong. Is it that we ain't doing things to please you? Or is it that the white folks is bothering you?" Before I could respond, she looked directly into my eyes and said, "I don told you we is with you all the way." Then her face became radiant and she said in words of quiet certainty, "But even if we ain't with you, God's

---

4. The evolving commitment by Dr. King to nonviolence was the topic of conversations in Los Angeles, March 20-26, 1993, between the author and the Rev. Glenn Smiley, who worked with Dr. King throughout the Montgomery boycott and afterward. The story of King's change of attitude toward guns is also found in Clayborne Carson's "The Unexpected Emergence of Martin Luther King, Jr.," *Stanford Report* (January 17, 1996) and in an abbreviated account by Carson, "The Boycott that Changed Dr. King's Life," *The New York Times Magazine* (January 7, 1996), 38.

gonna take care of you." As she spoke these consoling words, everything in me quivered and quickened with the pulsing tremor of raw energy.[5]

Despite continued opposition, mass arrests, and threats, the boycott remained nonviolent and unwavering in its determination to end segregated city buses. Thoroughly Gandhian, King stressed that the purpose of the boycott wasn't to drive the Montgomery Bus Company *out* of business but to put justice *in* business. They were not trying to defeat the enemy but to make possible a more inclusive opportunity for all of Montgomery's citizens. Preaching, singing, praying, and hands-on training equipped the people for their historic boycott that ended successfully on December 21, 1956 by order of the U.S. Supreme Court. In his first sermon at the beginning of the boycott, King had said:

> If you will protest courageously, and yet with dignity and Christian love, when the history books are written in future generations, the historians will have to pause and say, "There lived a great people—a black people—who injected new meaning and dignity into the veins of civilization." This is our challenge and our overwhelming responsibility.[6]

These words proved prescient as a new chapter of U.S. history was begun at Montgomery.

---

5. King, Jr. *Strength to Love*, 125.
6. King, Jr. *Stride Toward Freedom*, 63.

The Way of Nonviolence

It is crucial to note that the Montgomery Bus Boycott began with an appeal to Christian love as the way of protest exemplified in the Sermon on the Mount. Very quickly, however, the demands of the movement for justice and the need to devise various tactics in carrying out the boycott led increasingly to the teachings and example of Mohandas Gandhi and the Indian freedom movement. King began drawing upon his reading of Gandhi and his theoretical understanding of *satyagraha* (i.e., "truth force" or "soul force") and discovered it to be amazingly applicable to the civil rights movement and the quest for justice.

As King said again and again, while Jesus Christ furnished the spirit, the motivation for justice, Mahatma Gandhi provided a fresh and compelling *method* for working through the practical implications of that spiritual grounding. *Nonviolent resistance* was the key to overcoming evil with good. Gandhi had taught that the greatest power in the world is the power of truth found in every human being, every man and woman, no matter how poor or oppressed. Discovering this inner power and standing firm in it enables a person to rise with dignity and purpose and stand against evil and injustice. It is important to have a noble goal or end in view, but even more important, taught Gandhi, are the *means* used to achieve that end. Means and end are interrelated. In fact, the means used are the end in the process of becoming realized. Just as an apple seed will produce an apple tree, the fruit of justice will only come from the right seed being planted.

Nonviolent resistance is the means for achieving justice. But it is a way in which the innocent will suffer, just as Jesus did on the cross. Through the suffering of the innocent comes redemption. Despite the suffering, the servant of truth labors on, knowing that, as King put it, "the arc of the universe is long, but it bends toward justice." Justice in the Beloved Community will not subdue the defeated and create new oppression, but it will bring all together in a fellowship of reconciliation.

This Gandhian philosophy, blended with the biblical faith, became the undergirding force of the movement. As the boycott—and subsequent campaigns—unfolded, strategies and tactics were devised that were consistent with the way of nonviolence.

In Montgomery the boycott was centered in the churches, where frequent mass meetings were held. An ecumenical spirit brought people together across denominational lines, although very few white people participated. Class was minimized as people of varied economic conditions joined together. Boycotting the buses meant that people with cars helped form car pools that added to the solidarity across class lines.

The pattern of the church meetings fostered the spirit of nonviolence, with great singing, praying and preaching. The preaching was particularly used to inculcate the nonviolent spirit and the need to overcome evil with good and violence with nonviolence. Dr. King was superb in teaching Gandhi's philosophy of nonviolence as the methodology for applying Christian love in the struggle for justice. Within the framework of nonviolent resistance, people discovered the power for justice of traditional teachings about courage, endurance, humility, self-worth, goodwill, love, faith and hope. The struggle on the streets took these teachings out of the realm of generalities and pious utterances into the life and death struggle for social change in the Jim Crow South.

Music was a vital part of this movement. Since the days of slavery, black Christians had expressed their faith, their suffering, their determination and their hope through singing. As civil rights leader Dorothy Cotton put it, they were "singing their way to freedom." Traditional hymns and modern songs (especially from the labor movement) were put into the service of the movement with words created to reflect the struggle: "I've Been in the Storm So Long," "Freedom is A'Coming," "Which Side Are You On?" "Woke up This Morning With My Mind Stayed On Freedom" and "We Shall Overcome." Whether at prayer or in jubilation or marching into a phalanx of policemen with cattle prods and dogs, music gave purpose and strength and hope to the struggle.[1]

One evening, law enforcement officers came to Highlander Folk School in Tennessee, determined to find an excuse to close down the school. They made everyone get on the floor as they searched the premises. People began singing "We Shall Overcome" over and over. One young woman added a new verse, "We Are Not Afraid." And as the people took heart, the officers got more and more unsettled, finally leaving the school. Another time a sheriff and his deputies burst into a rural church near Albany, Georgia, parading around the sanctuary, threatening the worshipers and saying that their freedom movement was undermining

---

1. Dorothy Cotton, "Music, Soul, and Social Change," *Fellowship*, Vol. 61, No. 11-12 (November-December 1995), 19-20.

"the southern way of life." The frightened people began to sing quietly and yet with determination, "We'll Never Turn Back":

> We've been 'buked and we've been scorned
> We've been troubled sure as you're born
> But we'll never
> Turn back.
> No we'll never
> Turn back
> Until we walk in peace.

Unable to deal with such singing faith, the sheriff and his deputies turned on their heels and left the church. As Andrew Young observed,

> Somehow through the music a great secret was discovered: that black people, otherwise cowed, discouraged, and faced with innumerable and insuperable obstacles, could transcend all those difficulties and forge a new determination, a new faith and strength, when fortified with song. The music was not a political or economic gift to the people from the authorities, nor could it be taken away by them—music was the gift of the people to themselves, a bottomless reservoir of spiritual power.[2]

Music was indeed "a bottomless reservoir of spiritual power." Mahalia Jackson drew from that reservoir and watered the desert places so the weary could find rest and hope.

---

2. Young, *An Easy Burden*, 183.

On the wider national scene, in the years to come musicians would give creative and powerful expression to the challenge and meaning of the freedom movement that was taking place in the United States. Duke Ellington performed "King Fit the Battle of Alabam" at the Newport Jazz Festival, and he wrote an instrumental number, "Nonviolent Integration." Charlie Mingus composed "Freedom" and "Prayer for Passive Resistance." Lena Horne sang "Now!" to the Israeli tune "Hava Nagila," and Oscar Brown composed the "Freedom Now Suite: We Insist." Harry Belafonte gave enormous, ongoing support to the movement in every way possible. Sweet Honey in the Rock, a powerful and melodious group of black women, gave expression to the rich musical heritage of the black struggle for freedom. Folk singers like Pete Seeger, Joan Baez, Bob Dylan, Peter, Paul and Mary and countless others sang the message of the movement to the nation, on the streets and on the stage.

As the months of the boycott wore on, methods of nonviolence training were devised according to the need of the hour. As the hope of integrating the buses became more and more certain, a technique was developed as part of some of the meetings: Chairs would be lined up to simulate the seats on a bus. Participants in a role play would take the parts of driver, police, white passengers, black passengers. Through the role play they were able to experience various possible scenarios and test out their ability to carry out their objectives peacefully. It was the experience time and again that some of the most angry would learn to channel their anger into amazing, courageous nonviolent actions, thereby disproving the mistaken assumption that nonviolence is an expression of weakness and passivity. Andrew Young wisely observed, "People in the movement had very serious grievances and some of them were angry enough to kill if they were provoked. SCLC's way was to train people to channel that anger into constructive, nonviolent action. We always had to be on guard against those who would use individual rage to destroy the movement."[3] As Gandhi said, "Just as one must learn the art of killing in the training of violence, so one must learn the art of dying in the training for nonviolence." But, he warned, "Nonviolence cannot be taught to a person who fears to die and has no power of resistance."

The Montgomery Improvement Association developed a careful and effective boycott. Twenty-three dispatch centers were set up where people could get rides in vehicles made available, both by black taxi companies and individual owners. Some persons hitchhiked while many walked. When the City of Montgomery began efforts to get the car insurance of the boycott vehicles canceled, Lloyd's of London stepped forward to underwrite the insurance needs of the MIA.

As a result of the boycott, the bus company lost over a million dollars, and the head of the company had a heart attack. As word of this got reported at one of the mass meetings, a minister said "Our brother, head of the bus company, has had a bad heart attack. I think we should kneel right here and pray for his speedy and complete recovery." A chorus of "amens" followed his appeal and the worshipers knelt in prayer for their adversary.[4]

Rev. Smiley, at the request of Dr. King, drew up a list of suggestions for the movement to help prepare the people to move from the boycott to boarding what were going to be unsegregated buses. The first list contained general suggestions:

1. Not all white people are opposed to integrated buses. Accept goodwill on the part of many.

---

3. Young, *An Easy Burden,* 460.
4. Smiley, *Nonviolence,* 16-17.

2. The whole bus is now for the use of all people. Take a vacant seat.
3. Pray for guidance and commit yourself to complete nonviolence in word and action as you enter the bus.
4. Demonstrate the calm dignity of our Montgomery people in your actions.
5. In all things observe ordinary rules of courtesy and good behavior.
6. Remember that this is not a victory for Negroes alone, but for all Montgomery and the South. Do not boast! Do not brag!
7. Be quiet but friendly; proud, but not arrogant; joyous, but not boisterous.
8. Be loving enough to absorb evil and understanding enough to turn an enemy into a friend.

These were followed by specific suggestions:

1. The bus driver is in charge of the bus and has been instructed to obey the law. Assume that he will cooperate in helping you occupy any vacant seat.
2. Do not deliberately sit by a white person, unless there is no other seat.
3. In sitting down by a person, white or colored, say "May I" or "Pardon me" as you sit. This is a common courtesy.
4. If cursed, do not curse back. If pushed, do not push back. If struck, do not strike back, but evidence love and goodwill at all times.
5. In case of an incident, talk as little as possible, and always in a quiet tone. Do not get up from your seat! Report all serious incidents to the bus driver.
6. For the first few days try to get on the bus with a friend in whose nonviolence you have confidence. You can uphold one another by a glance or a prayer.

7. If another person is being molested, do not arise to go to his defense, but pray for the oppressor and use moral and spiritual force to carry on the struggle for justice.

8. According to your own ability and personality, do not be afraid to experiment with new and creative techniques for achieving reconciliation and social change.

9. If you feel you cannot take it, walk for another week or two. We have confidence in our people. GOD BLESS YOU ALL.

Just as Gandhi had called his autobiography *The Story of My Experiments with Truth,* one can trace throughout the civil rights movement experiments with Truth in each phase of the struggle, as they lived with the dynamic tension between the theory and the practical application.[5]

The evening of December 20, the night before the boarding of integrated buses was to take place under Supreme Court order, Dr. King spoke at two mass meetings. At both he held up the headlines from the morning edition of the Montgomery newspaper:

> TOMORROW IF NEGROES RIDE THE BUSES INTEGRATEDLY, THERE WILL BE BLOOD FLOWING, AND FIGHTING AT EVERY STREET CORNER.

"If this be true," said Dr. King, "then let us see to it that every drop of blood is our own and every act of fighting on the street corners is theirs." At the same time, Smiley was meeting with a group of white people, preparing them with nonviolence training, to help avert the predicted violence the next day.

Meeting with Dr. King late on the evening of December 21, Smiley said to him, "Dr. King, tomorrow I want to be

---

5. Above quotes and paragraphs taken from King, Jr., *Stride Toward Freedom,* 94-173.

paid, for I have been working here for a whole year with the Fellowship of Reconciliation paying my expenses, and now I think it is time to collect my salary." Knowing Glenn's great sense of humor, King smiled and said, "Name your price." Glenn said, "I want to be the first person to ride by you on an integrated bus in Montgomery, Alabama." King laughed and they both hugged at the end of a trying day.

At dawn the next day, Dr. King, Rev. Smiley, Rev. Abernathy, E. D. Nixon and Mrs. Bascum met at the bus stop and boarded the first bus that came, in the presence of some photographers and supporters. When they reached downtown, they were joined by Rev. Robert Graetz, a white minister of a black Lutheran church, and a few others.

In riding twenty-eight buses that day, Smiley wrote that things generally proceeded quite smoothly except for three acts of violence that he witnessed: a pregnant woman was shot in the leg by a sniper; a white woman on a bus rolled up a magazine and hit a black professor over the head, knocking off his hat and messing up his hair (he simply put his hat back on and continued reading the newspaper); and finally, a young white man hit a large black woman in the mouth, knocking her down. He then quickly got in a car and left.

Smiley came to help and said to her, "You didn't say a thing to him. Were you praying?"

"Quite the contrary. I wanted to cut him to ribbons."

"Why didn't you?" he asked.

"Well, because only last night I was able to tell myself and that little man (referring to Dr. King) that tomorrow if I am hit when I ride the bus, I am not going to hit back. But I really did want to cut him up."[6]

The historic boycott ended in true Gandhian fashion. Rivers of blood did not flow as predicted. People willingly took the violence upon themselves but did not inflict it.

---

6. Smiley, *Nonviolence*, 18-22.

The boycott ended on a note of reconciliation, emphasizing goodwill, politeness, and a continued nonviolent spirit.

Beyond Montgomery

The burgeoning civil rights movement grew and spread with many able leaders and spokespersons. Martin Luther King, Jr. however, came to be recognized as the leading interpreter, representative, and symbol of this people's movement. He was a spirit-led prophet, rooted in the Christian faith, inspired and informed by Gandhian nonviolence, with a keen sense of history and the rich possibilities — and weaknesses — of the American democratic experiment.

Although he had earlier felt drawn to an academic post where he could reflect, teach, and write, the Montgomery boycott set him on a different path that he would follow to the end, regardless of the consequences. He preached and lectured extensively and raised funds for the movement. After the boycott, Dexter Avenue Church gave Coretta and Martin King two thousand and five hundred dollars for a trip abroad, their first out of the country. The Montgomery Improvement Association gave another one thousand dollars, affirming appreciation and recognizing the Kings need for rest after the strenuous events of the past year.

They decided to go to Africa and on March 3 became part of a delegation going to the Gold Coast for independence celebrations. The delegation included Ralph Bunche, A. Philip Randolph and Adam Clayton Powell. They were especially welcomed by Prime Minister Kwame Nkrumah, who, on March 5, proclaimed at the polo grounds in Accra the end of British rule and the independence of the nation of Ghana. It was a historic moment as American descendants of slaves brought from Africa were honored guests in this land, whose descendants had been abducted and taken to America in chains. And Dr. King felt a special kinship with Nkrumah, who had led his own people in their nonviolent struggle for freedom.[1] King was a founder and first president of the Southern Christian Leadership Conference. He managed to find time to write a number of books, beginning with *Stride Toward Freedom*, and followed by *The Measure of a Man, Strength to Love, Why We Can't Wait, The Trumpet of Conscience*, and his last book, *Where Do We Go From Here: Chaos or Community?*

Upon their return from Africa, King was increasingly called on to speak and preach around the country. On May 17, he spoke at the culmination of the NAACP's Prayer Pilgrimage for Freedom as 37,000 persons from around the country gathered at the Lincoln Memorial. It was his first speech on the national stage and the gathering thundered their approval as he eloquently called for the right to vote. He began receiving honorary degrees from prestigious institutions, and at his alma mater, Morehouse College, as he received an honorary doctorate, Benjamin Mays said, "You are mature beyond your years, wiser at twenty-eight than most men at sixty; more courageous in a righteous struggle than most men can ever be; living a faith that most men preach about and never experience. . . . 'See,' said Emerson,

---

1. Miller, *Martin Luther King, Jr.*, 61.

'how the masses of men worry themselves into nameless graves when here and there a great soul forgets himself into immortality.' "[2]

In early 1958, King was able to finish his first book, *Stride Toward Freedom*. It was his stirring and profound account of the Montgomery bus boycott. In the same period the Fellowship of Reconciliation opened a regional office in Nashville, staffed by James Lawson, who was studying for the Methodist ministry at Vanderbilt University. Lawson, Glenn Smiley and Ralph Abernathy became a reconciliation team that held workshops and spoke in many states. They distributed the newly published FOR comic book, *Martin Luther King and the Montgomery Story*, which had been prepared in consultation with King and with a financial grant from the Fund for the Republic. Nearly a quarter of a million copies of the comic book were distributed, helping to spread to the grassroots the story of Montgomery and the power of nonviolence. FOR also distributed tens of thousands of a small brochure, *How to Practice Nonviolence*, as well as a new edition of Richard Gregg's classic, *The Power of Nonviolence*, that included a new chapter about the bus boycott and an introduction by King. Also in 1958, SCLC under the presidency of Dr. King launched its Crusade for Citizenship with the goal of doubling the number of Negro voters. Civil rights activities continued to spread. Sit-ins in Oklahoma City and Wichita, Kansas, by NAACP Youth Councils along with the Congress on Racial Equality (CORE) and FOR members started up, as did the Youth March for Integrated Schools led by Bayard Rustin. In September Martin and Coretta went to Recorder's Court to accompany Ralph and Juanita Abernathy who were there for Ralph to testify regarding a person who had assaulted him. A racist guard took offense at the Kings attempting to enter the court and suddenly grabbed Dr. King, twisted his arm behind

---

2. Miller, *Martin Luther King, Jr.,* 62.

his back and jailed him. Coretta was almost arrested as well by the angry guards, who called her "gal" when ordering her to leave. In the cell King was roughed up further, then eventually released on bond. When he appeared in court and was fined ten dollars for refusing to obey an officer, he said he could not pay a fine "for an act that I did not commit and above all for brutal treatment that I did not deserve." Awaiting jail, he was released when his fine was paid by white Commissioner Clyde Sellers, who said he would not allow the jail to be used for what he called a "publicity stunt."[3]

Later in that fateful month of September, King went to New York City for book signings of *Stride Toward Freedom*. While he was signing books at Blumstein's in Harlem, a deranged woman plunged a letter opener into his chest and beat on him as she shouted curses at him. His doctor told him he would have died if he had sneezed. At Harlem Hospital it took three surgeons three hours to remove the blade that was touching his aorta. When a school girl in White Plains, New York heard the story, she wrote Dr. King that she was so thankful he did not sneeze! King said he remembered her letter more than any other get-well message he received.

When King spoke to the press at the hospital ten days later, he said he bore no ill will toward Izola Curry, the woman who had stabbed him (she was later to be admitted to a state hospital for the criminally insane). In his statement to the press, King said that the stabbing "demonstrates that a climate of hatred and bitterness so permeates areas of our nation that inevitably deeds of extreme violence must erupt. Today it was I. Tomorrow it could be another leader or any man, woman or child who will be the victim of lawlessness and brutality."[4]

---

3. Miller, *Martin Luther King, Jr.*, 68-70.
4. Miller, *Martin Luther King, Jr.*, 72. King, Jr., "I See the promised Land," in *Testament of Hope*, 285.

Convalescing, King decided it was a good time to respond to a long-pending invitation from Prime Minister Jawaharlal Nehru for him to come visit India, the land of Gandhi. With financial assistance from the SCLC and the American Friends Service Committee, Coretta and Martin decided to go and were able to make the trip in February. They saw themselves coming not as tourists but as pilgrims, and they were deeply moved and impressed in what they saw. They met with the prime minister and with Vinoba Bhave, the walking saint, who went around India getting rich people to give land to the poor; it was called the *bhoodan* (land gift) movement. They visited the ashram at Sokhodeora where they met with Jayaprakash Narayan, a Gandhian advocate of *sarvodaya* or nonviolent socialism, the constructive program of social service and cooperatives. The Kings were struck by poor villagers working to build Gandhi's call for a decentralized, grass-roots democracy. They went to Shantiniketan, the "abode of peace" where the great poet Rabindranath Tagore lived and wrote. From the north of India, the Kings went to the south where they saw great Hindu temples and Christian churches going back to the dawn of Christianity. They went to *Gandigram* (Gandhi village) where they were greeted by five hundred members of the peace army or *Shanti Sena,* volunteers who worked to resolve conflict and build peace. They joined the worship of the volunteers who were dressed in plain white *khadi,* the homespun cloth Gandhi had advocated in building a self-reliant India. Texts were read from the sacred scriptures of the Hindus, Christians, Jews, Muslims and Buddhists, reflecting the approach of Gandhi, who recognized the validity of many paths to God. The Kings also visited villages of the outcastes, untouchables whom Gandhi had called *harijans,* children of God. As they traveled for four weeks all over India they were deeply touched by both the spirit and practice of Gandhian nonviolence. And not only were they there as pilgrims. They were received with joy and honored everywhere they went. Coretta was often called upon to sing and Martin to speak. At a press conference as they left, he called on India to take up the true spirit of Gandhi as a nation, to call for universal disarmament and to unilaterally disarm herself as an example for the world to follow.[5]

5. Miller, *Martin Luther King, Jr.*, 72-81.

The Sit-ins and the Freedom Rides

On November 29, 1959, Martin Luther King, Jr. announced to the congregation at the Dexter Avenue Baptist Church in Montgomery that, effective on the fourth Sunday of January, he would be leaving. He was needed in Atlanta where the offices of the Southern Christian Leadership Council were located. He told his parishioners, "History has thrust something upon me which I cannot turn away." It was difficult for him and the family to leave Dexter and Montgomery, but the time had come for the move. The next day, King said to the press that "the psychological moment has come when a concentrated drive against injustice can bring great, tangible gains." It was time, therefore, for a full-scale assault on segregation "in all its forms." "We must," he said, "train our youth and adult leaders in the techniques of social change through nonviolent resistance. We must employ new methods of struggle involving the masses of the people."[1]

---

1. Miller, *Martin Luther King, Jr.*, 84.

The significance of his prescient words was not long in coming. Joseph McNeill, a student at North Carolina Agricultural and Technical College in Greensboro, was refused service at the bus terminal lunch counter on January 31. His roommate, Ezell Blair, had read the FOR comic book, *Martin Luther King and the Montgomery Story*. When McNeill told Blair about the incident, they looked through the comic book and decided they should take up a nonviolent action. The next day, with two other students, they started a sit-in at the lunch counter of Woolworth's five-and-ten cent store. Refused service, they stayed for hours, then returned the next day. Others began to join them, including white students from Women's College in the town. A spark had been set—the psychological moment was there—and the student sit-ins spread across the South. By the end of March more than fifty cities were involved in a spontaneous grassroots movement. Nashville, which already had a strong base of students trained in nonviolence by Jim Lawson, naturally joined in the protests. In *motive,* the campus magazine of the Methodist Student Movement, Jameson Jones wrote:

> When called names, they keep quiet. When hit, they do not strike back. Even when hostile white youth pull hair and snuff out burning cigarettes on the backs of Negro girls, the girls do not retaliate. They pray and take what comes, in dignity.[2]

The sit-ins went on for months throughout the South. Attacks by hostile whites and stiff jail sentences did not deter them. In fact the protestors grew in strength and depth. In many places they carried with them the words, "Remem-

---

2. "Issues in the Sit-ins," *motive*, May 1960, quoted in Miller, *Martin Luther King, Jr.*, 89.

ber the teachings of Jesus Christ, Mahatma Gandhi, and Martin Luther King, Jr." They studied King's *Stride Toward Freedom* and Richard Gregg's *The Power of Nonviolence,* and they referred to training materials such as *Rules for Action* and "How to Practice Nonviolence."

At the suggestion of Ella Baker, SCLC called for a national conference of sit-in leaders. Two hundred and twelve persons came, mostly from the South but also from a few campuses in the North. King and Lawson were the keynote speakers and the conference followed King's suggestion of forming some kind of continuing organization. Thus was born the Student Nonviolent Coordinating Committee (SNCC) with a statement of purpose that said:

> We affirm the philosophical or religious ideal of nonviolence as the foundation of our purpose, the presupposition of our faith and the manner of our action. Nonviolence, as it grows from Judaic-Christian tradition seeks a social order of justice permeated by love. Integration of human endeavor represents the first step towards such a society.

The relentless tide of the sit-ins continued, and by August the Southern Regional Council issued a report stating that lunch-counter segregation had been abolished in twenty-seven Southern cities. Rev. Wyatt Tee Walker, newly appointed executive director of the SCLC in Atlanta, said that the results achieved in six months of sit-ins far outran what years of expensive litigation in the courts could have achieved. "Boycotts against stores are not putting them out of business," he said, "but bring them to the point of moral change." In King's address at the institute he stressed "an absolute commitment to a philosophy of non-injury and the way of love," expressing his deepening commitment as the challenges and demands were placed on him.

Showing his support of the sit-ins, King joined seventy-five Negro college students in Atlanta in sitting-in at Rich's department store. At his arrest, he said he would stay in jail ten years if that is what it took to end segregation at Rich's. Although the charges against King and students were dropped, King was arrested on October 25 for supposedly violating the probation he had been given for not having obtained a Georgia driver's license when he moved to the state. He was given four months of hard labor, put in leg irons and thrown in solitary confinement at Reidsville State Prison.

It was the time of the 1960 presidential election, and the nation was aroused by the civil rights struggle. Candidate Nixon had no comment on King's imprisonment and the grave dangers he faced isolated in a southern prison. But a Kennedy aide, Harris Wofford, moved quickly. Wofford, a lawyer, admirer of Gandhi and FOR member, got Senator John Kennedy to phone Mrs. King and offer his help. Robert Kennedy, the senator's campaign manager, called the judge involved and got King released on a two thousand dollar bond. Martin Luther King, Sr., whose politics were much more conservative than his son's, publicly endorsed Senator Kennedy as a result. King, Jr. chose not to endorse any candidate but rather to keep his prophetic freedom for the ongoing struggle.[3]

In the spring of 1961, it was decided to take the sit-ins "on the road" with Freedom Rides through the South challenging segregated interstate travel, just as the first Freedom Ride had done in 1947. James Farmer, the CORE director, informed President Kennedy about the new

---

3. Miller, *Martin Luther King, Jr.*, 86-106.

initiative, hoping to pressure the cautious administration into action.

On May 4, Trailways and Greyhound buses were boarded for the trip South. The freedom riders were on a dangerous mission and the costs were high. The first arrest was in Charlotte, North Carolina, but it was in Rock Hill, South Carolina, that things really got out of hand. A white gang pounced on the riders. John Lewis, a Negro divinity student and Albert Bigelow, a former Commander in the U.S. Navy, were both beaten to the ground without offering any resistance. On May 14 in Anniston, Alabama, the Greyhound bus was set upon with crowbars. Windows were knocked out, the tires punctured, and the bus was set on fire with an incendiary bomb. The riders were beaten as they came from the bus. The Rev. Fred Shuttlesworth brought cars to the scene to take the injured to the hospital in Birmingham. Although the FBI arrested nine white men for their part in the attack, they were either acquitted or the charges dropped. None were punished. Jim Crow "justice" prevailed.

The violence and arrests continued but the Freedom Rides did not stop. Mob violence took over in Birmingham and Montgomery and severe beatings of the black and white freedom riders were inflicted. In Montgomery the Justice Department's attorney, John Siegenthaler, and the Time-Life news bureau chief were beaten as well. Hundreds of U.S. marshals were brought in and the governor of Alabama, John Patterson, threatened to arrest them. At a mass meeting at Ralph Abernathy's church on the evening of May 20, over one thousand people showed up in support of the freedom riders. King spoke and laid responsibility with the governor. "The law may not be able to make a man love me, but it can keep him from lynching me," said King. A large mob of angry whites surrounded the church, threw stones and bottles through the sanctuary windows and kept the siege up throughout the night. Finally the governor gave in to strong pressure from Washington and had the national guard disperse the crowd.

By the fall, there were signs from the Interstate Commerce Commission on all buses and in the bus stations indicating that discrimination with regard to race, color, creed or national origin was against the law of the land. The Freedom Rides, following the sit-ins, had a powerful impact on the cause of desegregation and the future of the movement.

From November of 1961 to August of 1962, the Albany (Georgia) Movement sought to bring the power of the movement into this Deep South city. A long, protracted campaign aided by King ensued. Despite the time, energy and sacrifice it entailed, with many beatings and arrests as well as the dynamiting of the Shady Grove Baptist Church in nearby Leesburg, the Albany Movement failed to accomplish much that was tangible. Resistance to change had to be fought every step of the way, for segregation was supported by the dominant political, religious, cultural and economic institutions of society.

King went through a period of intense self-questioning and even considered withdrawing from his leadership in the movement. The impresario Sol Hurok made a tantalizing offer to make Martin Luther King his chief lecturer, speaking all over the world for a guaranteed minimum of one hundred thousand dollars a year. King rejected the offer and eventually moved through his uncertainty to renewed commitment to the people's struggle. God had touched his life, and he would not be unfaithful to the heavenly vision.[4]

---

4. Oates, *Let the Trumpet Sound*, 205.

The Birmingham Campaign

In 1963, the civil rights movement focused its forces on Birmingham, a place King called "probably the most thoroughly segregated city in the United States," a place with more unsolved bombings of homes and churches than anywhere else in the country, a city marked by terrible police brutality. Focusing on desegregating public accommodations, the campaign began with a sit-in on April 3, 1963. A final agreement to desegregate Birmingham was reached on May 10 between representatives of the white business community and the black community.

The SCLC decided to challenge segregation in Birmingham where the fiery and fearless Rev. Fred Shuttlesworth had led a small but powerful group of local black clergy to oppose racism in the city, organizing, among other things, an economic boycott of the downtown stores. Under King's leadership the Birmingham campaign was organized carefully. He drew upon the Citizenship Education Program in Dorchester, South Carolina, that Rev. Andrew Young and Dorothy Cotton had so effectively developed along Gandhian lines whereby campaigns followed four steps: investigation, communication, negotiation, confrontation and reconciliation.[1]

In addition to Young and Cotton and Rev. Bernard Lee, Rev. James Lawson along with Diane Nash and James Bevel were brought to Birmingham because of their experience in the Nashville movement that grew out of the workshops led by Lawson.

King had met Lawson at Oberlin in 1957 where Lawson was a seminary student working on his Master's in Religious Studies. The son of a Methodist minister, Lawson was a conscientious objector to war, who had served a one-year prison term for refusing to register for the draft during the Korean war. After prison he had gone to India as a Methodist missionary where he had studied Gandhian nonviolence. While in India, Lawson read about the Montgomery bus boycott, and he was inspired by the application of *satygraha* to America's racial problems. He remembered that Gandhi had told the well-known American minister and writer Howard Thurman that someday an American Negro would carry on his (Gandhi's) message; Lawson sensed that King was that man.

After India, Lawson entered seminary at Oberlin, where he met King who came to Oberlin to speak on campus. When Lawson and King met, there was an immediate attraction of minds and spirits. Both were twenty-eight years old, both articulate and charismatic, both committed to nonviolence. Although Lawson planned to get his degree at Oberlin and then work for his doctorate, King persuaded him to drop his plans and come South to help in the movement, which was spreading rapidly and desperately needed someone of Lawson's experience and ability to teach the theory and practice of nonviolence.

---

1. Young, *An Easy Burden,* 188-90.

The Fellowship of Reconciliation, with the aid of Glenn Smiley, appointed Lawson to do field work in Nashville, a city full of bright students and more amenable to change than deep south cities like Atlanta. Lawson and Smiley led nonviolence workshops around the South, but Lawson particularly concentrated on building a deeply committed, carefully trained student movement in Nashville. Out of his training arose a highly successful sit-in movement led by students who went on to become national leaders in the civil rights movement — persons like Bernard Lafayette, Diane Nash, James Bevel, Marion Berry and John Lewis.[2]

When the Birmingham campaign was planned, it was natural to draw upon the leadership from the Nashville sit-ins. SCLC knew Birmingham would be tough and therefore the plans were laid carefully. Nightly mass meetings brought the community together for inspiration and education, mental and spiritual preparation. Prayers and singing undergirded the message of the preachers. Regular church goers were well accustomed to "altar calls" in which sinners were called to come to the front and pledge their lives to Christ. Similarly altar calls were given to those who were ready to give their lives to serving Christ through the nonviolent campaign. They were asked to turn in any guns or knives and to rely solely upon the power of Truth. Scripture came alive with new meaning and challenge as they heard familiar texts such as Ephesians 6:13–18:

> Therefore take the whole armor of God, that you may be able to withstand in the evil day, and have done all, to stand. Stand therefore, having girded your loins with truth, and having put on the breastplate of righteousness, and having shod your feet with the equipment of the gospel of

---

2. For the full story of the King-Lawson friendship and the Nashville movement, see David Halberstam's *The Children* (New York: Random House, 1998).

peace; besides all these take the shield of faith,
with which you can quench all the flaming darts
of the evil one. And take the helmet of salvation,
and the sword of the Spirit, which is the word of
God. Pray at all times in the Spirit, with all prayer
and supplication.

Like Gandhi's *satyagrahi,* "votaries of truth," a nonviolent army was being raised up in Birmingham for the battle
ahead, an army "with no supplies but its sincerity, no uni-
form but its determination, no arsenal except its faith, no
currency but its conscience. It was an army that would
move but not maul. It was an army that would sing out but
not slay. It was an army that would flank but not falter. It
was an army to storm bastions of hatred, to lay siege to the
fortresses of segregation, to surround symbols of discrimination. It was an army whose allegiance was to God and
whose strategy and intelligence were the eloquently simple
dictates of conscience."[3]

Out of the mass meetings came the recruits for the campaign. A Leadership Training Committee set up screening
and training for those who volunteered. The training uti-
lized socio-dramas in which simulated situations anticipated the kind of experiences they would have during
demonstrations and marches and sit-ins. Role plays involving verbal and physical attacks by hostile police and
onlookers helped the leaders discern who were prepared to
go all the way in the campaign. Films helped to convey the
history of nonviolence campaigns. Especially useful were a
film on Gandhi and the freedom movement in India; "Walk
to Freedom," the story of the Montgomery bus boycott;
and an NBC documentary on the sit-ins in Nashville. Everyone in the campaign signed a commitment card that stated:

---

3. King, Jr., *Why We Can't Wait,* 62.

I HEREBY PLEDGE MYSELF—MY PERSON AND BODY—TO
THE NONVIOLENT MOVEMENT. THEREFORE I WILL
KEEP THE FOLLOWING TEN COMMANDMENTS:

1. MEDITATE daily on the teachings and life of Jesus.
2. REMEMBER always that the nonviolent movement in
   Birmingham seeks justice and reconciliation—not victory.
3. WALK and TALK in the manner of love, for God is love.
4. PRAY daily to be used by God in order that all men might
   be free.
5. SACRIFICE personal wishes in order that all men might be
   free.
6. OBSERVE with both friend and foe the ordinary rules of
   courtesy.
7. SEEK to perform regular service for others and for the
   world.
8. REFRAIN from the violence of fist, tongue, or heart.
9. STRIVE to be in good spiritual and bodily health.
10. FOLLOW the directions of the movement and of the
    captain of a demonstration.

I sign this pledge, having seriously considered what I do and with
the determination and will to persevere.

Name _____

Address _____

Phone_____

Nearest relative _____

Address _____

Besides demonstrations, I could also help the movement by:
(Circle the proper items)
Run errands, Drive my car, Fix food for volunteers, Clerical work,

Make phone calls, Answer phones, Mimeograph, Type, Print signs, Distribute leaflets.

ALABAMA CHRISTIAN MOVEMENT FOR HUMAN RIGHTS
Birmingham Affiliate of S.C.L.C.
505 1/2 North 17th Street
F. L. Shuttlesworth, President

The segregationists fought the campaign in every way possible, from court injunctions to heart-rending violence. Safety Commissioner "Bull" Connor, with his water cannons and police dogs, was determined to stop the movement in its tracks. He filled the jails, but still the movement returned, with hundreds upon hundreds of children joining in the assault against segregation. The nation watched in horror as Connor unleashed his savagery against the nonviolent protesters, showing the extent to which racists would go to oppose racial justice.

On Good Friday, King, with Ralph Abernathy and about fifty others, were arrested when they tried to begin a march across the street from their headquarters, the Sixteenth Street Baptist Church. They were quickly stopped by a large contingent of police, who came at them with police dogs and night sticks.

Behind bars, King wrote—on newspaper margins and on the back of legal papers — his "Letter from a Birmingham Jail" that has since become one of the great classics of prison literature. In it he answered a well-publicized statement that had just been released by eight "moderate" white clergymen — Protestant, Catholic and Jewish. They called the Birmingham campaign "unwise and untimely." They said the courts were the proper channel for challenging segregation and that they did not want outsiders coming in to destroy the peace of their city.

In response, Rev. King drew upon the ethical teachings of the Bible and the principles of democracy, carefully delineating the rationale and imperative for the civil rights revolution.

King wrote to the clergymen that he was compelled to go from his hometown with the gospel of freedom just as the apostle Paul had gone throughout the Greco-Roman world to proclaim the gospel. He challenged the very idea of the outsider with words he often used in his sermons:

> Injustice anywhere is a threat to justice everywhere. We are caught in an inescapable network of mutuality, tied in a single garment of destiny. Whatever affects one directly affects all indirectly.[4]

King asked the clergymen to look at the injustice behind the unrest and the demonstrations and the refusal of the white power structure to address the injustice facing the Negroes in the courts, in the unsolved bombings of Negro churches and homes, as well as the humiliation of segregation in Birmingham's stores. The clergy's call for negotiation simply ignored the good faith efforts to negotiate that had been spurned.

The alarms of the moderate clergy over civil disobedience ignored the distinction between just and unjust laws that goes back to the Bible itself. No less than Augustine said that "an unjust law is no law at all," a distinction biblically rooted in the belief that "we must obey God rather than man." In the Book of Daniel, Shadrach, Meshack and Abednago refused to obey Nebuchadnezzar, just as the first-century Christians were martyred because of their defiance of the Roman Empire. King reminded the clergy that Hitler acted *legally* in his nefarious deeds while the Hungarian freedom-fighters acted *illegally* in defying their communist tyrants. Aiding Jews

---

4. Washington, "Letter from Birmingham City Jail" in *Testament of Hope*, 290.

during the Nazi times was *illegal:* Were the resisters wrong to do so? And were Negroes wrong to defy crippling and vicious segregation statutes? Or are they following a higher law that all people of goodwill should accept?

King concluded his letter by appealing to the clergymen to look to the future in which both the Judaeo-Christian heritage and the tenets of democracy would vindicate the present challenge of the civil rights movement:

> One day the South will recognize its real heroes. They will be the James Merediths, courageously and with a majestic sense of purpose facing jeering and hostile mobs and the agonizing loneliness that characterizes the life of the pioneer. They will be old, oppressed, battered Negro women, symbolized in a seventy-two-year old woman of Montgomery, Alabama, who rose up with a sense of dignity and with her people decided not to ride segregated buses, and responded to one who inquired about her tiredness with ungrammatical profundity: "My feets is tired, but my soul is rested." They will be the young high school and college students, young ministers of the gospel and a host of their elders courageously and nonviolently sitting-in at lunch counters and willingly going to jail for conscience's sake. One day the South will know that when these disinherited children of God sat down at lunch counters they were in reality standing up for what is best in the American dream and the most sacred values in our Judaeo-Christian heritage, and thusly, carrying our whole nation back to those great wells of democracy which were dug deep by the Founding

Fathers in their formulation of the Constitution and the Declaration of Independence.[5]

On the afternoon of Easter Sunday, with King and many others in jail, a march was planned from the New Pilgrim Baptist Church to the city jail. Converging from a number of churches, upwards of five thousand persons, dressed in their finest Easter clothes, took part in the march. Two blocks from the jail their way was blocked by Police Commissioner Bull Connor and his forces, including fire trucks with high pressure hoses. Andy Young, at the head of the march, called on the people to pray. The mass of marchers dropped to their knees and began fervently praying and singing. After some minutes of prayer, one of the ministers rose and called upon the people to march to the jail.

As the people stood up and began marching slowly forward, some singing "I want Jesus to walk with me," Bull Connor yelled to the police to stop them and ordered the firemen to turn on the hoses. Amazingly, the police and firemen just stood and watched, as if they were transfixed. One old woman cried out as she moved toward the jail, "Great God Almighty done parted the Red Sea one mo'time!" When I heard Andy Young tell this story from the pulpit of Riverside Church in New York City, the congregation was awed at this example of the power of the powerless, of unarmed love overcoming armed hatred.

After King and Abernathy were released from jail on a three hundred dollar cash bond, a strategy session was held at the Gaston Motel in which it was decided to mobilize the Negro children of Birmingham. Jim Bevel, Dorothy Cotton, Bernard Lee and Andy Young went into the schools to

---

5. Washington, *Testament of Hope*, 302. This historic letter was smuggled out of the jail bit by bit. Nelson Mandela's autobiography, written during his long years of imprisonment, was hidden in coffee cans and buried in the prison yard to prevent its being confiscated. After Mandela's release, the precious manuscript became the basis of his monumental *Long Walk to Freedom. The Autobiography of Nelson Mandela.*

recruit the children. Sometimes the principals called the
police, but the recruiting continued nonetheless. Six thousand children, ages six to sixteen, volunteered and were
trained. On Thursday, May 2, after eating lunch in the
churches, the marching began. Dr. King and other SCLC
leaders spoke to the first contingent gathered at the Sixteenth Street Baptist Church. In groups of ten to fifty, the
children filed out of the church and headed for City Hall.
Mass arrests were made. When the police ran out of patrol
wagons, they started using school buses. Wave upon wave
of marchers were arrested. Three groups got as close as fifteen feet of the City Hall, but most were picked up almost
as soon as they left the church. When the children were
arrested they fell to their knees in prayer. Nine hundred
fifty-nine of them were arrested that Thursday. The next
day another assault was planned, but it faced a different
tactic by the police who sought to bar the children from
even leaving the church. Nearly five hundred children got
out nonetheless and were met with fire hoses and unleashed
police dogs. The savage scenes of children being knocked
down by water from high pressure hoses, and others being
bitten by police dogs, were telecast around the world, building sympathy for the movement and repugnance at the evil
of segregation.

On Sundays small groups of Negroes sought to worship in
white churches. Most were turned away but a few churches
welcomed them. The comedian and activist Dick Gregory
flew in from Chicago and on May 6 led still more children
who were ready to march. He carried a sign that said, "Everybody wants freedom" while the children chanted, "Don't
mind walking 'cause I want my freedom now." About one
thousand Negroes were arrested that Monday. Reportedly,
eight hundred children were kept in the jail yard for four
hours in the pouring rain and then shipped out in open
trucks. Those inside who protested were put in solitary

confinement. The girls were examined for venereal disease, with the same rubber gloves being used on everyone. People protesting against what was happening were beaten repeatedly. Girls who asked for aspirin were given laxatives and then put in cells without toilets. Others were forced to scrub the hallways with toothbrushes and steel wool.

The protests in the city continued but as tensions mounted violence broke out. In the face of police state tactics being used, the SCLC leaders were unable to keep order. Governor George Wallace sent in state troopers and the state highway patrol. Finally, the U.S. Justice Department and other government officials began to call for a negotiated settlement and exerted pressure on Birmingham's influential business leaders and industrialists to help move the city away from the brink. Finally, on May 10, a significant settlement was reached and bail funds were raised to get the remaining jailed protesters released.

The settlement provided for: 1) desegregation of lunch counters, fitting rooms, rest rooms and drinking fountains in all downtown stores within ninety days; 2) the placement of Negroes in previously all-white sales and clerical positions within sixty days; 3) the release of prisoners; and 4) firm establishment of communication between white and black leaders.

King called upon everyone now to move from protest to reconciliation. But even as the settlement portended tangible hope for the birth of a new Birmingham, the violence continued. A rally of the Ku Klux Klan was held, and the home of A. D. King (Martin's brother) and the Gaston Motel were dynamited. Fighting, rioting and looting broke out around the city and it took intensive work by the SCLC leaders and other people of goodwill to finally restore Birmingham to calm and to compliance with the settlement.[6]

6. Miller, *Martin Luther King, Jr.,* 130-152.

The success of the Birmingham campaign helped create a public groundswell that moved President John Kennedy and especially Attorney General Robert Kennedy to strongly support the aims of the movement. It started the momentum for the Civil Rights Act. After Birmingham, the Rev. Glenn Smiley called Dr. King "the best and freshest thing that ever happened in America, not just in Negro life, but in American life."[7]

It cannot be emphasized too much that King's twin emphases on the Judaeo-Christian heritage and the democratic heritage as "one nation under God, with liberty and justice for all" gave immense spiritual, moral and civic appeal to the ultimate goal of the civil rights movement. God and country were invoked in calling for the highest and best in human nature and potential, or as President Jimmy Carter was later to say, King "spoke of the America that never has been, of the America we hope will be."[8] King had a profound, deep faith in the potential of democracy to be inclusive, just, and free. His was not a patriotism of the "my country, right or wrong" variety, but a love of country that called it to live up to its highest possibilities. As outraged as he was by racism, he never advocated that his people should return to Africa or set up a separate black state, nor did he accept black separatism and isolation. He saw everyone as citizens of "a city set on a hill," a "not yet" that beckons us on nonetheless. His leading a nonviolent movement of high moral appeal, courageous action, and creative protest that included civil disobedience helped to reawaken a prosperous and imperial nation to its revolutionary beginnings and pristine democratic longings for a world freed of all oppression.

---

7. King, Jr., "Letter from a Birmingham Jail," in *Why We Can't Wait,* 60-64; cf Oates, *Let the Trumpet Sound,* 243.
8. President Jimmy Carter, January 1979, when Carter gave the first call for making Dr. King's birth date a national holiday.

The founders of the United States put in its founding document: "We hold these truths to be self-evident, that *all* men are created equal and endowed by their Creator with certain inalienable rights, among them life, liberty and the pursuit of happiness." The civil rights movement forced the United States to look at itself anew and discover the radical, universal inclusiveness of that little word *all,* a task that must be undertaken anew by each generation of those who cherish freedom and justice.

The success in Birmingham sparked numerous campaigns across the South. President Kennedy, in a nationally televised address in June 1963, finally threw the weight of his administration behind the freedom movement. Echoing King, the president called desegregation primarily a moral issue, "as old as the Scriptures and as dear as the American Constitution." Kennedy said that the United States was founded "on the principle that all men are created equal, and that the rights of every man are diminished when the rights of one man are threatened."[9]

---

9. Oates, *Let the Trumpet Sound,* 244-45.

On the National Stage

Washington D.C.

On August 28, 1963 the March on Washington for Jobs and Freedom took place, bringing 250,000 persons to the nation's capital to join in what King called "the greatest demonstration for freedom in the history of our nation." The August 28 march came on the heels of a growing momentum of vast public events that summer. Twenty-five thousand had gathered in Los Angeles and ten thousand in Chicago. In June, King spoke before 125,000 at a highly successful Freedom Walk in Detroit, held on the twentieth anniversary of a tragic race riot there in 1943.[1]

The director of the march was A. Philip Randolph, at seventy-four the elder statesman of the civil rights movement. Founder of the Brotherhood of Sleeping Car Porters in 1925, a time when blacks could not even join railway unions, Randolph was a pioneer in labor and civil rights issues. He had first planned a march on Washington in 1941

---

1. Miller, *Martin Luther King, Jr.*, 156.

to call for jobs for blacks in defense industries. President Franklin Roosevelt was able to get him to call off the march by issuing an executive order stating that there would be no discrimination in defense jobs or in government based on race, creed, color, or national origin. Roosevelt also agreed to establish the Fair Employment Practices Committee.

By the summer of 1963 the idea of a March on Washington was reborn in response to the gathering momentum of the civil rights movement, the violent resistance to the movement and the continuing legacy of racism in the country. Over a hundred civil rights, labor and religious organizations came together in a bold "coalition of conscience" with A. Philip Randolph at its head and Bayard Rustin as the deputy director. At first President Kennedy tried to get the organizers to call off the march, fearing violence in the streets and the undermining of his efforts to get the civil rights bill passed. In the end, however, meeting with the determined unity of the coalition, Kennedy endorsed the march.

Under the sure and meticulous planning of Bayard Rustin, the March on Washington was a resounding success; the fear of violence evaporated as the determined, nonviolent marchers descended on the nation's capital. They came from everywhere in thirty "freedom trains" and two thousand chartered "freedom buses." The sixty thousand white people among the 250,000 were an encouraging sign of the changing attitudes in the country.

The rally at the Lincoln Memorial was a dazzling gathering of celebrities, national leaders, singers, veterans of the movement, and thousands upon thousands of people from around the country. As the comedian Dick Gregory put it, "The last time I saw so many of us together Bull Connor was doing all the talking." Ralph Bunche and Burt Lancaster came from Paris with a scroll of support signed by fifteen hundred Americans. One hundred and fifty members of

Congress were there as were Lena Horne, James Baldwin, Marlon Brando, and Jackie Robinson. Odetta sang "Oh, Freedom," Peter, Paul and Mary contributed "If I had a hammer" and Bob Dylan "A bullet from the back of a bush took Medgar Evers' blood." Mahalia Jackson sang "I Been 'Buked and I Been Scorned" and Joan Baez "We Shall Overcome." A. Philip Randolph led off the speakers, calling the gathering "the advance guard of a massive moral revolution for jobs and freedom. This revolution reverberates throughout the land, touching every city, every town, every village where black men are segregated, oppressed and exploited." His practical wisdom is so easily forgotten: "The plain and simple fact is that until we went into the streets the Federal Government was indifferent to our demands."[2] Presiding over the rally, Randolph introduced some of the women leaders of the struggle: Diane Nash, married to James Bevel; Rosa Parks; Merlie Evers, wife of Medgar Evers, the Mississippi state secretary of the NAACP, who was shot in the back in the driveway of his home in Jackson; Gloria Richardson; and the widow of Herbert Lee of Liberty, Mississippi, who was shot by a state legislator for his voter registration work.

Eugene Carson Blake spoke, representing the Commission on Religion and Race of the National Council of Churches. Dr. Blake was the Moderator of the United Presbyterian Church in the U.S.A. and later was to become the general secretary of the World Council of Churches. His presence indicated the growing commitment of the mainstream churches to the freedom movement. In his pointed remarks he offered repentance for the racism of the churches of America and said to those in the freedom movement, "Alone and without us you have mirrored the spirit of

2. Miller, *Martin Luther King, Jr.*, 162.

Jesus Christ; you have offered your bodies to jail, to fire hoses, to dogs and, some of you, to death."

There was a behind-the-scenes crisis as leaders of the March worked to get John Lewis to tone down the forcefulness of his planned speech. Finally Randolph persuaded him to do so and only minutes before he rose to speak, Lewis revised portions of his speech. Nonetheless Lewis—born into harsh poverty in rural Alabama, arrested twenty-two times, savagely beaten twelve times — spoke words that needed to be said: "We are tired of being beaten by policemen. We are tired of seeing our people locked up in jail over and over again! And then you holler 'Be patient.' How long can we be patient? We want our freedom and we want it now! We do not want to go to jail, but we will go to jail if this is the price we must pay for love, brotherhood and true peace. . . . By the force of our demands, we shall splinter the segregated South into a thousand pieces, and put them back together in the image of God and democracy."[3]

King's "I Have a Dream" speech at the conclusion of the rally brought the day's events to a climax that awed the nation. The great orator of the civil rights movement delivered an address that has become one of the most memorable in U.S. history. After lifting up the continuing injustices and indignities facing the Negro in America, and the determination not to turn back until freedom is won, he said:

> I say to you, my friends that even though we must face the difficulties of today and tomorrow I still have a dream. It is a dream deeply rooted in the American dream that one day this nation will rise up and live out the true meaning of its creed — we hold these truths to be self-evident, that all men are created equal.

---

3. Williams, *Eyes on the Prize*, 197-202; Miller, *Martin Luther King, Jr.*, 160-162.

I have a dream that one day on the red hills of Georgia, sons of former slaves and sons of former slave-owners will be able to sit down together at the table of brotherhood.

I have a dream that one day, even the state of Mississippi, a state sweltering with the heat of injustice, sweltering with the heat of oppression, will be transformed into an oasis of freedom and justice.

I have a dream that my four little children will one day live in a nation where they will not be judged by the color of their skin but by the content of their character. I have a dream today!

I have a dream that one day, down in Alabama, with its vicious racists, with its governor having his lips dripping with the words of interposition and nullification, that one day, right there in Alabama, little black boys and black girls will be able to join hands with little white boys and white girls as sisters and brothers. I have a dream today!

I have a dream that one day every valley shall be exalted, every hill and mountain shall be made low, the rough places shall be made plain, and the crooked places shall be made straight and the glory of the Lord will be revealed and all flesh shall see it together.

This is our hope. This is the faith that I go back to the South with.

With this faith we will be able to hew out of the mountain of despair a stone of hope. With this faith we will be able to transform the jangling discords of our nation into a beautiful symphony of brotherhood.[4]

---

4. Washington, "I Have a Dream" in *Testament of Hope,* 217-220.

After the rally, its leaders went to the White House to meet with President Kennedy. Afterwards the president issued a statement saying, "One cannot help but be impressed with the deep fervor and the quiet dignity that characterizes the thousands who have gathered in the nation's capital to demonstrate their faith and confidence in our democratic form of government." Furthermore, he said that his Administration would "continue its efforts to obtain increased employment and to eliminate discrimination in employment practices."[5]

Birmingham

The March on Washington called the nation to its highest ideals and furthered the determination to keep marching until freedom was won. Yet, on September 15, a little over two weeks after the March on Washington, its afterglow was shattered when a bomb exploded at the Sixteenth Street Baptist Church in Birmingham, killing four girls who were in church that day. At Sunday school their lesson had been "The Love that Forgives." The kindergarten prayer that day was "Dear God, we are sorry for the times we were so unkind." It was Youth Day, and the four girls—Denise McNair (age eleven), Cynthia Wesley, Carole Robertson, and Addie Mae Collins (all age fourteen)—had left Sunday school early to participate in the worship service honoring the young people. They were putting on their choir robes when the dynamite went off, killing them, injuring others, and blowing out the face of Jesus in a stained glass window.

The pastor of the church, the Rev. John Cross, helped rescuers pull away the debris where they found the slain girls.

---

5. Miller, *Martn Luther King, Jr.,* 167.

A fifth, Addie Mae's eleven-year-old sister, Sarah, was found alive.

In a moving eulogy at the girls' funeral, King offered comfort to the bereaved families and the eight thousand mourners who gathered for the service. He also lifted up the great faith imperatives of the nonviolent freedom movement, saying "in spite of the darkness of this hour we must not despair. We must not become bitter; nor must we harbor the desire to retaliate with violence. We must not lose faith in our white brothers. Somehow we must believe that the most misguided among them can learn to respect the dignity and worth of all human personality." And he said of the four girls,

> They did not die in vain. God still has a way of wringing good out of evil. History has proven over and over again that unmerited suffering is redemptive. The innocent blood of these little girls may well serve as the redemptive force that will bring new light to this dark city. The holy Scripture says, "A little child shall lead them." The death of these little children may lead our whole Southland from the low road of man's inhumanity to man to the high road of peace and brotherhood. These tragic deaths may lead our nation to substitute an aristocracy of character for an aristocracy of color. The spilt blood of these innocent girls may cause the whole citizenry of Birmingham to transform the negative extremes of a dark past into the positive extremes of a bright future. Indeed, this tragic event may cause the white South to come to terms with its conscience.[6]

---

6. Washington, "Eulogy for the Martyred Children," in *Testament of Hope*, 221-223.

King's belief in the redeeming power of unearned suffering was a recurrent theme of his to a movement that faced daily trials and hardships. The leaders of the civil rights struggle were slandered and labeled traitors, fomenters of violence, lawless agitators, communists. Their homes and churches were bombed, their families threatened, their lives in constant danger. And these sufferings were faced not only by the leaders but by everyone participating in the movement. Many lost their jobs, some had to move from their community. They faced arrest and beating, cattle prods and attacks by police dogs. Protestors — "black and white together," women and men, the old and the young, the rich and the poor — paid the harsh price of redeeming a sick, racist society. The gospel hymn that asked "Must Jesus bear the cross alone and all the world go free?" reflected their experience in the next line: "No, there's a cross for everyone, a cross for you and me."

King, ever the pastor, helped people rise above bitterness and fear to find meaning in their suffering, knowing that God would comfort and sustain them no matter what. God would provide "the inner equilibrium to stand tall amid the trials and burdens of life," making "a way out of no way," and transforming "dark yesterdays into bright tomorrows."[7]

The nation's price for freedom

These beliefs were sorely tested as violence spread across the country. On November 22, President John F. Kennedy was struck down by an assassin's bullet while in a motorcade in Dallas, Texas. Reacting in shock when he heard the news, King told his wife, "This is exactly what is going to

---

7. Washington, "Our God Is Able" in *Testament of Hope,* 509.

happen to me. I told you, this is such a sick society. I don't expect to survive this revolution."[8] Whatever premonitions he had, he continued undeterred. He had set his hands to the plow and would not turn back.

In the SCLC Newsletter he observed, "The shot that came from the five-story building cannot be easily dismissed as the isolated act of a madman. Honesty impels us to look beyond the demented mind that executed this dastardly act. While the question 'who killed President Kennedy?' is important, the question 'what killed him?' is more important. Our late President was assassinated by a morally inclement climate. It is a climate filled with heavy torrents of false accusation, jostling winds of hatred and raging storms of violence . . . this virus of hate that has seeped into the veins of our nation, if unchecked, will lead inevitably to our moral and spiritual doom."[9]

In a land where it is easier to get a gun than a driver's license, the tumultuous sixties saw the murder of one public figure after another. Before the decade had ended, Medgar Evers, John Kennedy, Malcolm X, Robert Kennedy and Martin King would all be felled by assassins' bullets. Change was coming, but the price was woefully high.

Florida

The tragedy of the Kennedy assassination did not stop the civil rights movement, but it was a foreboding of the violence yet to come. Great change was taking place but not without great resistance. In 1964, King marched in the demonstrations in St. Augustine, Florida calling for the integration of public facilities there. On Easter Sunday nine women were arrested

---

8. Letter to author from Mrs. King, August 2, 1999.
9. "Epitaph and Challenge," SCLC Newsletter, November-December 1963, page 1, quoted in Miller, *Martin Luther King, Jr.*, 175.

in the segregated dining room of the Monson Motor Court in St. Augustine. Among the interracial group of women was the mother of Massachusetts Governor Endicott Peabody, and the wife of the first Negro bishop in the Episcopal church. Prior to the arrest, Mrs. Peabody—who also was the wife of a retired Episcopal bishop—along with two other women had sought to receive communion at the Trinity Episcopal Church. The church, to prevent such an unseemly event, had simply canceled the communion service, and the women were barred by seven men of the vestry from even entering the sanctuary! The rector's comment to the press was that they were simply trying to protect life and property.

The oldest town in the United States, St. Augustine — founded in 1565 — was a small city whose main revenue was tourism and one of its featured sites was the old Slave Market. St. Augustine was so racist that when students staged a sit-in at a lunch counter there they were locked inside and cruelly beaten by Klan members. A local Negro dentist, Dr. R. N. Hayling, was active in the NAACP. He and three other Negroes were abducted by the Ku Klux Klan and beaten until they were unconscious. One of the crowd looking on yelled, "Work on his right hand. He's a right-handed dentist!" The sheriff was tipped off and arrived in time to prevent the four men from being set afire with gasoline and burned to death.

On May 26, civil rights marches to the Slave Market were planned. The marchers were met by a white mob carrying chains and pipes. When they knelt to pray, someone yelled, "Niggers ain't got no God!" The police allowed the mob to attack the Negroes, and one NBC television cameraman had to be hospitalized after being attacked with a chain. The violence continued in subsequent marches, causing King to call St. Augustine "the most lawless community that we've ever worked in [during] the whole struggle over the last few years." People arrested were herded into deplorable, overcrowded cells, and it took a court injunction and one hundred state troopers for the marches to continue, still in the face of ongoing violence. At one rally at the Slave Market, Hosea Williams said, "We may die but we'll die with this in our mind — if the black man loses his freedom, no man will be free. We will bleed and die that America shall be free."[10] As the Negroes hummed the song "We Love Everybody," Williams prayed for "our white brethren." In response to a counter march by Klansmen through the Negro section of town, a sign welcomed them, "Peace and Brotherhood to you."

Sixteen rabbis came to St. Augustine to join a march through a white neighborhood and the next day they went with nine Negroes to the Monson Motor Lodge where they were arrested. The marches continued as did savage violence with support from the white power structure of the city and the state. Finally, however, in late June a biracial committee was set up, and integration began to come to the city. On July 2, Martin Luther King and other civil rights leaders were invited to the White House as President Johnson signed the Civil Rights Act of 1964.[11]

Mississippi

That summer brought black and white volunteers from all over the country to Mississippi to participate in Mississippi Freedom Summer with the goal of registering black voters. The previous summer's assassination of NAACP leader Medgar Evers was indicative of the violent resistance to the freedom movement in Mississippi.

10.Miller, *Martin Luther King, Jr.,* 183-191.
11.Miller, *Martin Luther King, Jr.,* 192-195.

Three of the volunteers for Freedom Summer — James Chaney, Andrew Goodman and Michael Schwerner—disappeared. On August 4, they were found murdered near Philadelphia, Mississippi. Nonetheless, segregation was crumbling. Fannie Lou Hamer and the Mississippi Freedom Democratic Party challenged the seating of the all-white Mississippi delegation to the National Democratic Convention. Their very presence and prominence would have been unthinkable only a few years earlier. Even though their efforts were crushed at the Convention, this was a portent of the coming political power of blacks in the South.

Allan Knight Chalmers from Boston University School of Theology (King's alma mater) went to Mississippi that summer. Seeing his northern license plate, a Mississippi state patrolman stopped Chalmers and lectured him about "outside agitators" coming down and upsetting the Southern way of life. "I'll tell you this," said the patrolman, "Mississippi will never integrate." "How long is never?" asked Chalmers. Taken aback, the patrolman thought a few moments and then said, "Twenty-five years." Chalmers observed, "Once you've taken away your opponent's hope of victory, he is already defeated."[12]

And Beyond

In September, King and Ralph Abernathy went to West Berlin at the invitation of Mayor Willy Brandt. Dr. King then proceeded to the Vatican for an audience with Pope Paul VI. The year, which began with King's being named "Man of the

---

12. Class discussion at Boston University School of Theology, 1964. In 1998, the South Africa Council of Churches invited New Testament scholar Walter Wink and me to South Africa to lead workshops on nonviolence at a time of great discouragement in the anti-apartheid movement (the government had declared a national emergency and was coming down mercilessly on its critics). Although the situation was bleak, the anti-apartheid movement was strong. Sensing the desperation behind the government's cruel policies, an old woman in the workshop said, "We have a saying in Soweto, 'The dying horse kicks the hardest just before it dies.'" Her analogy was right: apartheid was dying.

Year" by Time magazine, culminated with the Nobel Peace Prize being awarded to him on December 10, 1964. At thirty-five, he was the youngest ever to receive the award.

On the way to Oslo, King preached to a huge throng at St. Paul's Cathedral in London—the first non-Anglican to preach from its historic pulpit. When King received the gold medallion, he received it on behalf of all the movement, not just the leaders but the thousands upon thousands of "ordinary" persons — sharecroppers, domestic servants, teachers, students, laborers, office workers—who had risked their jobs, their homes, even their lives, in the harsh struggle for freedom. The price had been high but, in the words of the freedom hymn, they had kept "their eyes on the prize." Appropriately, King gave all the money for the prize to the civil rights movement.

King's acceptance speech was not limited to civil rights; it included his vision for peace and justice in the world and the means to this goal:

> Nonviolence is the answer to the crucial political and moral questions of our time — the need for man to overcome oppression and violence without resorting to violence and oppression.[13]

After King received the prize, he was received and honored by dignitaries throughout Europe. It was a sober reminder of the temper of the times at home, however, that he was ignored by U.S. ambassadors on the continent. The hostility to King generated by the FBI was increasing even as his stature grew throughout the world.[14] Nonetheless, the Nobel Award solidly confirmed Martin Luther King, Jr. as a world prophet whose message of nonviolence resonated in the hearts of people everywhere.

---

13. Washington, "Nobel Prize Acceptance Speech," in *Testament of Hope*, 224.
14. Young, *An Easy Burden*, 320-326.

Marching from Selma
to Montgomery

In 1965 Selma, Alabama became the focus of the effort to secure voting rights for African-Americans. A slave market during the days of slavery, Selma was as opposed to integration as had been Birmingham, or better "Bombingham" as it came to be known. Even though its population was half black, only one per cent of its black population was registered to vote. But, despite severe repression — with lynchings and bombings and unchecked violence—Selma's black citizens were building a protest movement in the city. Mass meetings, sit-ins and other forms of protest were developing there, especially following the success of the Birmingham campaign and the March on Washington.

Under the slogan "One Man, One Vote," concentrated efforts for voter registration were growing. Those who came to the Dallas County Courthouse to register faced the determined resistance of the town authorities, who went to great lengths to keep the voter rolls as lily white as possible. Absurdly difficult literacy tests were given to African-Americans who tried to register, whereas white registrants, even if they could hardly write their own names, were given no such tests. If Birmingham had Police Commissioner Bull Connor, Selma had Sheriff Jim Clark, who was just as ruthless and violent as Connor. With his cattle prods, police dogs and night sticks, he met attempts at exercising basic fundamental rights—such as the right of assembly and the right to vote—with swift retaliation.

The Civil Rights Act of 1964 unfortunately did not translate into the universal right of suffrage. The right to vote had to be fought for every step of the way, especially in states like Alabama where governor George Wallace believed in "segregation today, segregation tomorrow, segregation forever." With such powerful white resistance in Selma, a delegation of black citizens appealed to Dr. King to come help them secure the right to vote. This resulted in SCLC's involvement beginning in January 1965, on the 102d anniversary of President Lincoln's Emancipation Proclamation. At a mass meeting in Selma's Brown Chapel African Methodist Episcopal Church, Dr. King kicked off the campaign with strong participation and leadership given by the local black community. This was followed by a march on the courthouse on January 18, led by Dr. King and John Lewis, SNCC chairman. While there were no arrests that day, subsequent marches led to so many that as the jail filled the prisoners were placed in a fenced compound and then taken to the county work farm. The next march Dr. King led in Selma was later that same week when he led over one hundred teachers to the courthouse. It was a breakthrough for these professionals to publicly march and get arrested, because generally teachers had been hesitant to risk their jobs and reputations challenging white authority. It was also significant because it dramatized how ludicrous it was for teachers to be arrested for simply trying to register to vote.[1]

---

1. John Lewis, *Marching With the Wind,* (New York: Simon and Schuster, 1998), 301-315.

The momentum built and, as in Birmingham, children were marching and getting arrested by the hundreds. Unlike Birmingham, which had a united hard-line leadership against the civil rights movement, Selma had some moderate leaders, including its mayor and public safety director, who were embarrassed, even appalled, by Clark's storm trooper tactics. In mid-February, Sheriff Clark was hospitalized from exhaustion. Black schoolchildren came to the hospital and prayed for his recovery. One of their signs said, "Get well soon, in mind and body." When he was released, however, he ignored their loving witness, choosing instead to wear a sign of his own: "Never."[2]

Once again on the front lines, Clark was as pugnacious as ever. On February 16 he was on the courthouse steps meeting that day's marchers. The Rev. C. T. Vivian, a stalwart from the Nashville and Birmingham campaigns and the Freedom Rides, was at the front, and he compared Clark and his deputies to the Nazis, with the television cameras recording the event. Clark socked Vivian in the mouth, knocking him down and then had him arrested. Once again the nightly news around the world graphically showed the brute force facing the civil rights efforts in Selma. Two days later in nearby Marion, a night march was held. During the march the street lights went out and the marchers and the press that were present were brutally attacked. Jimmie Lee Jackson, a young black man in the march, tried to protect his eighty-two-year-old grandfather and his mother in the melee that followed. A state trooper shot him in the stomach and he died a few days later.[3]

King, along with his close friend Rev. Ralph Abernathy, had been arrested in a march on February 1. Behind bars, the two ministers settled into their now established pattern of fasting, prayer, meditation, hymn singing, and exercise.

2. Lewis, *Marching*, 315.
3. Lewis, *Marching*, 315.

Less than two months after receiving the Nobel Peace Prize, King wrote a public letter from jail. In it he said:

> Why are we in jail? Have you ever been required to answer one hundred questions on government, some abstruse even to a political science specialist, merely to vote? Have you ever stood in line with over a hundred others and after waiting an entire day seen less than ten given the qualifying test? THIS IS SELMA, ALABAMA. THERE ARE MORE NEGROES IN JAIL WITH ME THAN THERE ARE ON THE VOTING ROLLS.[4]

While King was in jail, Malcolm X came to Selma on February 4 and spoke at a rally at the Brown Chapel where Coretta Scott King and Fred Shuttlesworth were speaking. He told Mrs. King that he had come to help, saying that if white folks realized that his ways were the alternative to King's, they would be more willing to listen to her husband, for whereas King had always stressed nonviolence and reconciliation, Malcolm X had ridiculed nonviolence as passivity and advocated the use of any means necessary to secure justice.[5] Tragically, on February 21, Malcolm X was gunned down in New York City as he was speaking at the Audubon Ballroom. It is important to remember that Malcolm's thought was evolving and maturing, as was Martin's. Malcolm X had recently gone to Mecca and had been profoundly influenced by that experience, returning to the United States stressing the universal message of Islam and respect of all persons regardless of their color.

The campaign continued, with King in and out of Selma. On Sunday, March 7, 1965, a fifty-four-mile march was

---

4. Oates, *Let the Trumpet Sound*, 339-340.
5. Conversation with Coretta Scott King in Atlanta, July 24, 1990 at a faculty meeting of the 15th Annual Summer Workshop on Nonviolence, The Martin Luther King, Jr. Center for Nonviolent Social Change, Inc.

Washington, DC, August 28, 1963. March on Washington for Jobs and Freedom. The occasion of the "I Have a Dream" speech.
©John C. Goodwin. Used with permission.

Arlington National Cemetery, February 6, 1968 during a march and prayer ceremony. L to R: Dr. King, Rev. Ralph Abernathy, unknown man, Rabbi Maurice Eisendrath, Rabbi Abraham Heschel. ©John C. Goodwin. Used with permission.

New York City, April 15, 1967. Mobilization march and demonstration against the war in Vietnam. Dr. Benjamin Spoke marching alongside Dr. King. ©John C. Goodwin. Used with permission.

Arlington National Cemetery, February 6, 1968 during a march and prayer ceremony.
L to R: Rabbi Abraham Heschel, Dr. King, Rabbi Maurice Eisendrath holding the Torah, Rabbi Everett
Gendler, Andrew Young. Rev. Jesse Jackson is partially hidden behind the Torah.
©John C. Goodwin. Used with permission.

New York City, April 4, 1967 (one year to the day before Dr. King was assassinated). Dr. King is answer-
ing questions at a press conference.
©John C. Goodwin. Used with permission.

Arlington National Cemetery, February 6, 1968.
©John C. Goodwin. Used with permission.

MARTIN LUTHER KING, JR.
JAN. 15, 1929 ——— APR. 4, 1968
FOUNDING PRESIDENT
SOUTHERN CHRISTIAN LEADERSHIP CONFERENCE
THEY SAID ONE TO ANOTHER,
BEHOLD, HERE COMETH THE DREAMER...
LET US SLAY HIM...
AND WE SHALL SEE WHAT WILL BECOME OF HIS DREAMS.
GENESIS 37: 19 - 20
RALPH DAVID ABERNATHY, PRESIDENT

Lorraine Motel, Memphis, Tennessee. Wreath in front of the room where Martin Luther King, Jr. was staying and the place he was shot.
Mary Ruth Robinson. Used with permission.

planned from Selma to the state capitol in Montgomery to petition Governor George Wallace to call an end to police brutality and allow the Negroes of Alabama to vote. While King was preaching that day in Atlanta, over five hundred gathered at Brown Chapel. They proceeded to the Edmund Pettis Bridge that spanned the Alabama River where they would begin to march down Highway 80. At the bridge, they were met by a phalanx of highway patrolmen wearing gas masks and bearing truncheons. The state police charged into the marchers hitting everyone in sight with billy clubs, bull whips and rubber tubing wrapped in barbed wire. They even charged into a church where some Negroes had sought to find refuge. They threw a young man through the church's stained glass window that depicted Jesus, the Good Shepherd. In the end, seventy Negroes were hospitalized and another seventy were treated for injuries in what has come to be remembered as "Bloody Sunday."[6]

On the heels of Bloody Sunday there was a groundswell of demonstrations across the country calling for the passage of a voting rights act. King sent out a national call for clergy to come to Selma and to march the following Tuesday, March 9. Like Gandhi, King had an uncanny ability to discern the importance of dramatic events and powerful symbols. Like Gandhi's Salt March to the sea to protest against the salt tax that hurt the poor, King called clergy of all faiths to come and march where their black brothers and sisters had been struck down. This would shock the nation into action. The response was electrifying. Overnight four hundred ministers, priests, nuns, and rabbis descended on Selma. The march was officially banned, and federal officials urged King to call it off. But his conscience would not allow him to turn the people back now. Speaking to fifteen hundred gathered at Brown Chapel he told them, "I do not

---

6. Lewis, *Marching*, 317.

know what lies ahead of us. There may be beatings, jailings, and tear gas. But I would rather die on the highways of Alabama than make a butchery of my conscience. There is nothing more tragic in all this world than to know right and not do it. I cannot stand in the midst of all these glaring evils and not take a stand."[7]

He led the marchers to the same place where Bloody Sunday had occurred two days earlier. Met by state troopers, they were ordered to disperse. King responded, saying that they wanted to pray. In the prayers that followed one Methodist bishop from Washington, D.C., compared this to the exodus from Egypt and asked God once again to part the Red Sea. When he finished, the troopers, as if in answer to his prayer, stepped aside, leaving the way open. However, King—fearing a trap—led the marchers back to the church, saying that they would continue their fight in the courts. That night, one of the ministers who had come to Selma, the Unitarian James Reeb, was clubbed to death by white bigots.

As Kennedy had been galvanized by events in Birmingham, President Lyndon Johnson was outraged by Selma. He went before Congress to call for a voting-rights bill without delay or compromise. In the most impassioned speech of his presidency—John Lewis called it "probably the strongest speech any American president has ever made on the subject of civil rights"[8]—President Johnson said:

> At times history and fate meet at a single time in a single place to shape a turning point in man's unending search for freedom. So it was at Lexington and Concord. So it was a century ago at Appomattox. So it was last week in Selma, Alabama. . . .

7. Oates, *Let the Trumpet Sound*, 351.
8. Lewis, *Marching*, 339.

Rarely in any time does an issue lay bare the secret heart of America itself. The issue of equal rights for American Negroes is such an issue. And should we defeat every enemy, and should we double our wealth and conquer the stars and still be unequal to this issue, then we will have failed as a people and as a nation. . . .

Even if we pass this bill, the Battle will not be over. What happened in Selma is part of a far larger movement which reaches into every section and state of America. It is the effort of American Negroes to secure for themselves the full blessings of American life.

All the more important because he was a southerner, Johnson said in conclusion,

Their cause must be our cause too. Because it's not just Negroes, but really it's all of us who must overcome the crippling legacy of bigotry and injustice.

He then ended his address saying:

And we shall overcome.[9]

The president had invited Dr. King to sit in the Senate gallery during the address, but King, ever the pastor, remained in Selma to conduct the service for the slain James Reeb.

On the heels of Johnson's address, the courts approved the Selma-to-Montgomery march and ordered Alabama officials not to interfere. On March 21, thirty-five hundred persons — including celebrities from across the nation — gathered for the march under the protection of the

---

9. Williams, *Eyes on the Prize,* 278.

federalized Alabama National Guard. Only three hundred were allowed to march the entire way, because the four lane highway narrowed to two lanes for much of the route.

The march included representatives of the major civil rights organizations, religious groups and labor unions. Andrew Young, one of the key organizers, asked a contingent of Catholic nuns to be sure and wear their habits, because "nobody's likely to shoot at us if we have nuns in habits with us."[10]

Like the March on Washington, the Selma-to-Montgomery March involved incredible planning, detail and follow through. Thousands of people from around the nation had come to participate. Endless details were involved, like the route of march, encampments along the way, tents and food for the participants, security, communications. And there were only a few days to get ready. John Lewis paints a graphic picture of the logistics and people needed:

> Walkie-talkies, flashlights, pots and pans and stoves for cooking . . . the list went on and on. And so did the manpower. A crew of twelve ministers — we called them the "fish and loaves committee" — was responsible for transporting food to each campsite each evening. Ten local women cooked the evening meals in church kitchens in Selma. Ten others made sandwiches around the clock. Squads of doctors and nurses from the same Medical Committee for Human Rights that had provided the physicians who tended the wounded on Bloody Sunday now geared up for a different kind of casualty, with dozens of cases of rubbing alcohol and hundreds

---

10. Young, *An Easy Burden*, 363.

of boxes of Band-Aids, for the marchers' sore muscles and blistered feet.[11]

The marchers slept at campsites with tents erected on land owned by Negroes along the route. The National Council of Churches provided food, and the Medical Committee for Human Rights took care of medical needs. Somehow, as Andy Young reflected, "despite confusion, lack of schedule, rain, tragedy, absence of sufficient resources, whatever the obstacles — they served only to remind all of us that it is possible to do unbelievable things if people are determined enough."[12]

One of the marchers was the Dutch priest Henri Nouwen, who was then studying at the Menninger Clinic in Topeka, Kansas. Getting in his little Volkswagen, he drove to Selma. Picking up a black hitchhiker outside of Vicksburg, Mississippi — a risky thing for both passengers in the Deep South during that time — the twenty-year-old man named Charles exclaimed , "God has heard my prayer. He sent you as an angel from heaven. I've been standing here for hours and nobody would pick me up. The white man only wants to run at me and push me off the road. When you hitchhike you take your life in your hands, but I want to go to Selma. I made a cross in the sand with my stick, and I prayed to God that he would bring me to Selma to help my people. He heard my prayer."[13]

The March was a fervent, holy pilgrimage, an expression of the faith of a people who would not turn back. Like the Israelites wandering in the wilderness, the marchers risked everything on the journey to Freedom Land. They were "walking the walk," all the way to Montgomery. Rabbi Abraham Joshua Heschel best expressed it when he said, "I

---

11. Lewis, *Walking with the Wind*, 342.
12. Young, *An Easy Burden*, 366.
13. Henri Nouwen, *The Road to Peace*, edited by John Dear (Maryknoll, NY: Orbis Press, 1998), 76.

felt as if my legs were praying." Heschel wrote in his diary, "I thought of having walked with Hasidic rabbis on various occasions. I felt a sense of the holy in what I was doing. Dr. King expressed several times his appreciation. He said, 'I cannot tell you how much your presence means to us. . . .' Dr. King said to me this was the greatest day of his life and the most important civil rights demonstration. I felt again what I had been thinking for years: the Jewish religious institutions have missed a great opportunity — namely, to interpret a civil rights movement in terms of Judaism. The vast majority of Jews participating actively in it weren't aware of what the movement means in terms of the prophetic tradition."[14]

Henri Nouwen said that God's gift of song kept the march nonviolent. Anger was channeled into determination with new words made up to old melodies:

> I'm gonna cool it when the Spirit says, "Cool it."
> I'm gonna cool it when the Spirit says, "Cool it."
> When the Spirit says, "Cool it," I'm gonna cool it,
> O Lord.
> And I'm gonna bow when the Spirit says bow.

The final night of the march was at the City of St. Jude, a large Catholic complex for blacks not far from Montgomery that included a hospital and church. At great personal risk, the rector offered hospitality to the marchers. Under threat of excommunication, the rector and the Sisters of St. Jude defied their bishop, who had forbidden them to participate in the march. Archbishop Toolen had even asked for all outside priests and members of religious orders to leave Alabama. Claiming solidarity with the governor, Toolen

---

14. Susannah Heschel, "Abraham Heschel and Martin Luther King, Jr.," *Fellowship*, Vol. 64, No. 1-2 (January/February, 1998), 4-5.

said they were interfering with the internal affairs of his archdiocese and of the state.[15]

Over twenty thousand people gathered that evening for a four-hour outdoor concert organized by Harry Belafonte. The entertainers included such luminaries as Sammy Davis, Jr., Dick Gregory, Peter, Paul and Mary, Joan Baez, Leonard Bernstein, Tony Bennett, Ossie Davis and Odetta.[16]

As the march approached Montgomery, the U.S. Justice Department warned that there was a sniper in the outskirts of Montgomery prepared to assassinate Dr. King and that he should drop out of the march. He absolutely refused and continued on in the front of the line of march. Andy Young, figuring that most white folks had trouble telling Negroes apart, had an inspired idea. Without telling anyone why, he asked all the ministers in the march who had blue suits like Dr. King's to wear them and march alongside him as they came into Montgomery. There were around fifteen who gladly complied and the march proceeded without incident.[17]

As they entered Montgomery — "the cradle of the Confederacy" as it was called — tens of thousands joined in the final miles to the State Capitol, just across the street from the Dexter Avenue Baptist Church where King had been pastor during the Montgomery Boycott. While the great dome of the Capitol had above it the flags of Alabama and the Confederacy, the march came in behind scores of American flags like a victorious multitude overcoming the bastion of segregation.

Ten years after that Boycott had begun, another great milestone had been reached on the road to freedom. Ralph Abernathy introduced the final speaker, saying, "When

---

15. Henri Nouwen, *The Road to Peace*, 86.
16. Lewis, *Marching*, 345.
17. Young, *An Easy Burden*, 367.

God's people are in trouble, he sends them a leader: Martin Luther King, the greatest leader of this century, the Moses who is leading us through the wilderness to the land of freedom."[18] In his stirring speech, Martin Luther King, Jr. said that, despite all the suffering and killing, they would not turn back, they were on the move. Asking "How long will it take?" he answered:

> Not long, because no lie can live forever. How long? Not long, because you will reap what you sow. How long? Not long, because the arm of the moral universe is long but it bends toward justice. How long? Not long, cause mine eyes have seen the glory of the coming of the Lord, trampling out the vintage where the grapes of wrath are stored. He hath loosed the fateful lightning of his terrible swift sword. His truth is marching on. Oh, be swift, my soul, to answer Him. Be jubilant, my feet. Our God is marching on.[19]

As often happened, the successful climax of a campaign was followed by wanton and senseless violence. This happened after the exhilaration of the march to Montgomery. That night the marchers returned to Selma. One of the drivers was Viola Liuzzo, a white woman from Detroit, who had come to help with the march after seeing it on television. As she was driving back on Highway 80 with a young Negro, Leroy Moton, the car was ambushed. She was shot in the head and killed instantly as the car swerved off the road and crashed. The white racists came back to see what they had done. Moton pretended he too was dead and so his life was spared. At the Twenty-Fifth Anniversary of the March on Washington, I met the family of Viola. They were dressed

---

18. Nouwen, *The Road to Peace*, 91.
19. Washington, "Our God is Marching On," in *Testament of Hope*, 230.

in T-shirts identifying themselves as the family of Viola Liuzzo. Deeply proud of her, they attended such events in order to help keep alive the memory of her sacrifice for equal rights in this country.

Only a few months after the march from Selma to Montgomery, the U.S. Congress passed the Voting Rights Act, and on August 6, 1965, President Johnson signed it, laying the foundation for a sea of change in the politics of the South. As more and more blacks were able to vote, more blacks were elected to public office and more whites running for office no longer ignored the needs and concerns of the black community.

Carrying the Movement North

After Selma, King refused to rest on his laurels. He felt the movement had to go North to deal with the racial injustice there. "Freedom is not given, it is won by struggle," he would say again and again. Racism took a different form in the North, but it was rife there in the squalid slums, avaricious landlords, restricted neighborhoods, poor schools, and lack of job opportunities. The South had made great gains in civil rights. "In the North on the other hand, the Negro's repellent slum life was altered not for the better but for the worse. Oppression in the ghetto intensified. . . . School segregation did not abate but increased. Above all unemployment for Negroes swelled and remained unaffected by general economic expansion."[1]

The campaigns in the North began in Chicago with a challenge to racially segregated housing and what King called "the violence of poverty." Although his origins were middle class, King strongly identified with those in poverty. In early 1966, King (joined later by Coretta and their

---

1. Washington, "Next Stop: The North" in *Testament of Hope,* 189.

children) moved into a slum apartment to show solidarity with the poor. The poor paid *more* for worse housing than was paid for better apartments outside the slums, just as the poor were charged more for goods and services than residents in the suburbs. King visited the churches, the unions, the city officials. He talked long into the night with gang members, listening to their stories, their struggles, their hopes. He explained to them the nature of nonviolence and the power to change evil into good. The gang members were greatly impressed by King and agreed to support the nonviolent movement. Nonviolence workshops with gangs were organized, giving the young new hands-on experience in the tactics and strategy of nonviolence. The workshops included a film of the upheaval in Watts, where fifty Negroes had died and where the same police were still in power. This they contrasted with Selma where substantial changes for good resulted from the nonviolent approach. "That's the difference," said SCLC staffer Jim Bevel, "between a riot and thinking."[2] The efforts in the North were, however, more complex, and the results were more ambiguous.

Chicago Mayor Richard Daley spoke against these "outsiders" coming to his city, just as the clergy of Birmingham had done. He sought to counter their efforts by a number of highly publicized efforts to deal with the slums and poverty. Although these efforts seemed largely cosmetic, Daley's political skill and patronage undercut some of King's appeal. Marches in Chicago were smaller and the resistance more hostile and violent than had been anticipated. Forty thousand marched during a July 10 Freedom Sunday, with Dr. King nailing black demands on the door of city hall. At a later, much smaller march into segregated Marquette Park, they were met by an angry mob that

---

2. Oates, *Let the Trumpet Sound*, 392.

included George Lincoln Rockwell, head of the American Nazi party, and some men in their Ku Klux Klan robes. Stoned in the mêlée that followed, King said he had never experienced such hate, even in the worst moments in the South. Nonetheless, a Summit Agreement for fair housing was reached in August following negotiations with municipal, business and labor leaders. It was an important but partial victory.[3] King called the agreement "the most significant program ever conceived to make open housing a reality in a metropolitan area."[4]

3. Ralph David Abernathy, *And the Walls Came Tumbling Down* (New York: Harper & Row Publishers, 1989), 362-399.
4. Miller, *Martin Luther King, Jr.*, 251.

White Backlash, Black Power,
and the War in Vietnam

The times were increasingly tumultuous. The widening
war in Vietnam was bitterly dividing the country. The fight
against racism and economic exploitation was producing a
white backlash on the one hand and the call for black power
on the other. King agreed with certain aspects of the black
power movement. He sympathized with those who
responded in despair to the oppression by white power and
the white establishment's failure to enforce civil rights laws.
He agreed with the emphasis of the black power advocates on
gaining political and economic strength to achieve legitimate
goals and of building racial pride and accomplishment. But
he was firm in believing that hope not despair would fuel
revolutionary change.

King rejected the advocacy of separatism and violence as
futile and self-defeating. Going it alone would not strengthen
the movement, it would weaken it. Alliances with others is
not weakness but the potential for power. "There is no separate black path to power and fulfillment that does not

intersect white roots, and there is no separate white path to power and fulfillment, short of social disaster, that does not share that power with black aspirations for freedom and human dignity. We are tied together in a single garment of destiny."[1] The Beloved Community is an inclusive one. "We have come too far down the path now to turn back. There have been too many hymns of hope, too many anthems of expectation, too many deaths, too many dark days of standing over graves of those who fought for integration for us to turn back now. We must still sing, 'Black and White Together, We Shall Overcome.' "[2]

Nor would he compromise on nonviolence. He pointed out that fewer had died in ten years of nonviolent campaigns in the South than had during the three nights of rioting in Watts. "Darkness cannot drive out darkness, only light can do that. Hate cannot drive out hate: only love can do that." What the world needed, said King, was not for blacks to imitate the violence of their opponents but rather to strive to create "a new man" with "a new kind of power."[3]

King's decision to come out publicly and forcefully against the war in Vietnam was exceedingly controversial. Many of his black allies opposed it, saying that it would split and weaken the movement. Ralph Bunche, Roy Wilkins, Jackie Robinson, Senator Edward Brooke, Witney Young, the NAACP — all publicly criticized King. President Johnson, who had embraced King and the movement in his efforts for a Great Society, turned away from King in fury. But King could not oppose violence at home and remain silent about violence abroad, where entire Vietnamese villages were being destroyed in what he called "one of history's most cruel and senseless wars." He was deeply moved by the outspoken Vietnamese Buddhist monk, Thich Nhat

---

1. King, Jr., "A New Kind of Power," *The Progressive* (June 1967), 17.
2. SCLC staff retreat, 14 November 1966, quoted by Oates in *Let the Trumpet Sound*, 421.
3. King, Jr., "A New Kind of Power," *The Progressive* (June 1967), 17.

Hanh, whose speaking and writing about the war put an intensely human face on the suffering of the Vietnamese (in 1967, King would nominate the monk for the Nobel Peace Prize). Coretta, already publicly on record against the war, was a strong support for Martin. The well-known "baby doctor" Benjamin Spock hailed King as "the most important symbol for peace in this country."

In early 1967, King began devoting full speeches to the war, and on April 4 — exactly a year before he was murdered—he delivered a major address on the subject to a packed audience at Riverside Church in New York City. In Vietnam twice as many black soldiers as white soldiers were fighting and dying. The U.S. was spending $332,000 for every enemy killed in Vietnam, while it was spending $53 for every person in its "war" on poverty. What if those resources used in killing were being used to eliminate poverty? He spoke of "the cruel irony of watching Negro and white boys on TV screens, as they kill and die together for a nation that has been unable to seat them together in the same schools."[4] As a Christian minister he spoke of the tragedy of the impoverished Vietnamese people suffering through nearly three decades of war. "We must find new ways," he said, "to speak for peace in Vietnam and justice throughout the developing world—a world that borders on our doors. If we do not act we shall surely be dragged down the long dark and shameful corridors of time reserved for those who possess power without compassion, might without morality, and strength without sight."[5]

The reaction to the speech was swift and highly critical. Many of his allies in the civil rights struggle, black and white, took him to task for providing comfort to the enemy and splitting the civil rights movement. Deeply hurt by the criticism, King had nonetheless spoken the truth as

4. Washington, "A Time to Break Silence," in *Testament of Hope*, 233.
5. Washington, "A Time to Break Silence," in *Testament of Hope*, 231-233.

faithfully as he could. Having won the Nobel Peace Prize in 1964, he could not escape seeing the peace issue from a *world* perspective. In response to his critics, he said, "I have worked too long and too hard now against segregated public accommodations to end up segregating my moral concern. Justice is indivisible . . . it would be rather absurd to work passionately and unremittingly for integrated schools and not be concerned about the survival of a world in which to be integrated."[6]

King's harshest critics were those advocating a separatist path to black power, using any means necessary, and those supporting U.S. policies in Vietnam, whatever means were necessary to win the widening war. Both critics came up against the theological approach of King which was universal in its grounding and vision, beyond any one race, any one nation.

---

6. King, Jr., "Conscience and the Vietnam War," in *The Trumpet of Conscience,* 24.

Martin King's Humor

King was serious but not solemn, and he had a delightful sense of humor. He loved teasing and joking with those he was close to, especially his family and staff, and his sermons were often sprinkled with funny stories and humorous twists to important points. King knew the importance of humor for softening the blows of life and making them endurable. He knew that humor could reach people when perhaps nothing else would. And he knew the wisdom of Gandhi, who said that without a sense of humor he would have long ago committed suicide.

Ralph Abernathy wrote about King's "unflagging capacity to have fun and make everyone else join in."[1] Andrew Young, one of King's closest friends and co-workers, said,

> He teased, he could crack on you, insult you until the whole room was laughing 'til they cried. But it was never in anger, never in bitterness, it was always in fun. Martin wouldn't have teased

---

1. Abernathy, *And the Walls Came Tumbling Down*, 467.

anyone he didn't love. He could only relax that
way with people he trusted, his closest colleagues
and personal friends. An example of this is the
time when he ribbed Ralph Abernathy, calling
him the unrivaled president of the National
Association for the Advancement of Eating
Chicken.[2]

In his preaching he could put serious things in a way that
brought a smile to those who were in the audience, such as
saying that maybe opponents of the civil rights movement
had a point in claiming that you can't legislate morality;
nonetheless, he would say that even if the law couldn't
make white folks love Negroes, the law could at least keep
them from lynching Negroes. Laughter and clapping
erupted in the audience when he would make this point, or
when he quoted an old slave who said, "We ain't what we
ought to be and we ain't what we want to be and we ain't
what we're going to be. But thank God we ain't what we
was." King would say he had so many injunctions against
himself that he paid no attention to them, since he was
"enjoined January 15, 1929, when I was born in the United
States a Negro."

King really laughed when he heard that during the
Montgomery boycott, a large, strong Negro was insulted by
the bus driver when he tried to board. He said to the driver,
"I want you to know two things. One. I ain't no boy. And
two, I ain't one of those Martin Luther King nonviolent
Negroes."[3]

And King could even find humor in the midst of frighten-
ing events. At the time of the march in Mississippi after
James Meridith was shot, a particularly dangerous situation
developed, for in that state whites could act against

2. Young, *An Easy Burden*, 329-332.
3. Oates, *Let the Trumpet Sound*, 253, 281.

Negroes with impunity. At a rally held in Philadelphia, Mississippi, commemorating the murder of Goodman, Chaney and Schwerner, King called on Abernathy to pray. Filled with grief, he could still jokingly recall, "Since I wasn't about to close my eyes, Ralph prayed, but he prayed with a wary eye open."[4]

---

4. Young, *An Easy Burden,* 401.

A Revolution of Values:
The Triple Evils Confronted

As the war in Vietnam continued to escalate, King criss-crossed the country with his peace message. He was under constant surveillance by the FBI. Its director, J. Edgar Hoover, called Dr. King "a traitor to his country and to his race." A successful voter registration drive was launched in Cleveland that summer, but in other cities across the country rioting and burning took place, including four destructive days in Detroit that took forty-three lives and fifty million dollars in property. The massive spending on the war and the neglect of needs at home fueled such acts of fury and despair.

King, brooding on the desperate situation in the country, increasingly placed it within the context of a world of rising expectations in the face of age-old injustices. In this "world house," the triple interrelated evils of racism, materialism and militarism are to be found. The civil rights movement focused on racism, but it must not ignore the materialism of a society where the few have much and the many have little.

King again echoed Gandhi who said that God has given the world enough for everyone's need but not enough for everyone's greed. Although there are ample resources in the world to meet humanity's basic needs, the will and commitment have been lacking to build a just world. "The time has come," said King, "for an all-out war against poverty. The rich must use their vast resources of wealth to develop the underdeveloped, school the unschooled and feed the unfed."[1] Such a war against poverty, however, cannot ignore the militarism in a world where rich and poor nations alike are groaning under the weight of runaway arms budgets. The best minds are being employed to develop ever greater weapons of mass destruction and other lethal ways of killing. Although world leaders talk of peace, they are blind to the utter necessity of using peaceful means to achieve a peaceful end.

The war in Vietnam vividly demonstrated the folly of the world's richest nation using massive destructive power against one of the world's poorest nations. Not only had the U.S. not been able to conquer that tiny country, but in the process it undermined the struggle at home against poverty and racism, making a mockery of the peaceful, democratic ideals it proclaims to the world.

What was really needed was a "revolution of values to accompany the scientific and freedom struggles engulfing the earth."[2] The Cold War had derailed the U.S. from this needed revolution. Traditional capitalism and communism had each presented themselves as the answer to the world's problems and divided the world into allies and adversaries, with the accompanying unending arms race and ideological struggle that deflected it from solving the grave ills that beset the human family. But both offered only partial solutions. Capitalism overemphasizing the individual and the

---

1. King, Jr., *Chaos or Community*, 207.
2. King, Jr., *Chaos or Community*, 216.

profit motive, leading to cut-throat competition and unbridled materialism, with the few having great luxury while the gap between the rich and poor widens. Communism, instead, overemphasizing the collective and in the process robbing the individual of freedom, idolized the state.

Individualism and collectivism are both half truths, King argued. "Capitalism fails to realize that life is social" while "communism fails to realize that life is personal." What we need is "a socially conscious democracy, which reconciles the truths of individualism and collectivism."[3] Achieving this goal would require an unrelenting struggle against racism, materialism and militarism and a commitment to freedom, equality and justice, not for ourselves alone but for the whole human family, the "world house." And King felt certain that we could do this: "There is nothing to keep us from remolding a recalcitrant status quo with bruised hands until we have fashioned it into a brotherhood."[4] We must choose: chaos or community.

As prophetic and significant as King's call for a revolution of values was, he did not include among the interrelated evils that of sexism. Despite outstanding women in the movement — such as Rosa Parks, Coretta Scott King, Dorothy Cotton, Septima Clark, Ella Baker—on this issue King was a man of his time, who failed to evince a willingness to battle sexism as he did racism, classism and militarism. It is interesting to speculate how his views would have changed had he lived longer. Because of his openness to criticism and his practice of self-examination, he would surely have continued to grow in searching out the implications of revolutionary nonviolence. Not only sexism but homophobia and environmental degradation would doubtless in time have come to be seen as evils intrinsic to

---

3. King, Jr., *Chaos or Community*, 217.
4. King, Jr., *Chaos or Community*, 220.

what the New Testament scholar Walter Wink calls "the domination system."

The Beloved Community

For King, humanity's ultimate aim is the Beloved Community, embracing the whole human family under God, who is the loving, creative purpose at the heart of the universe. All are created in the image of God, "tied in a single garment of destiny."[1] Although King was firmly grounded in and committed to the Christian faith, his growing world vision also opened up his religious understanding. Thus in his final book, *Where Do We Go From Here? Chaos or Community?* he refers to love as "the key that unlocks the door which leads to ultimate reality."[2] Love is "that force which all the great religions have seen as the supreme unifying principle" the "Hindu-Moslem-Christian-Jewish-Buddhist belief" found in 1 John 4:7, 8, 12:

> Let us love one another; for love is of God, and everyone that loves is born of God, and knows God. He who does not love does not know God,

---

1. King, Jr., "A New Kind of Power," in *The Progressive* (June 1967), 17.
2. Page 223.

> for God is love. . . . If we love one another, God
> abides in us and his love is perfected in us.

For King, as for Gandhi, means and ends are intimately
interrelated: We must therefore use means that are in har-
mony with the end we are seeking. Separatism cannot produce unity, hate cannot lead to love, falsehood cannot lead
to truth, violence cannot bring nonviolence. We reap what
we sow.

The only way out, the only way forward, is through love:
love of God and love of neighbor. This is the ancient teaching of the prophets and, as Jesus made clear, this love
reaches out to include the enemy. King made certain that
his hearers did not confuse the meaning of "love" with
"like." Nor even with the varieties of things that are called
"love." The Greek words in the Bible that clarify this are
eros, philos and *agape.* Love in the biblical sense is *agape,*
self-giving love that sees the other as God sees him or her,
that works for the best in him or her. The love of *agape* is far
greater than romantic love, *eros;* and it is greater than love
between friends, *philos. Agape* is creative, redemptive
goodwill, extended to those we may not like, even to those
doing us harm.

Because humanity has rejected this approach as unrealis-
tic, we have lost our way. The world is an armed camp;
instead of providing for the basic needs of the vast majority
of humanity — jobs, food, shelter, health care — our
resources worldwide are being poured into weapons of
destruction, ways of killing instead of enhancing life. King
reminded America of the biblical injunction to beat swords
into plowshares and spears into pruning hooks. Our choice
is between nonviolence and non-existence.

The urgent need now is to apply nonviolence to every
area of life. Just as we have nonviolently, valiantly struggled
for racial justice, we should apply nonviolence to all fields of

human endeavor, including that of relations between nations. Nonviolence should be taught in our schools and religious communities.

If we are to survive, we must learn to face even our enemies and say,

> We shall match your capacity to inflict suffering by our capacity to endure suffering. We will meet your physical force with soul force. Do to us what you will and we will still love you. We cannot in all good conscience obey your unjust laws and abide by the unjust system, because noncooperation with evil is as much a moral obligation as is cooperation with good, and so throw us in jail and we will still love you. Bomb our homes and threaten our children, and, as difficult as it is, we will still love you. . . . But be assured that we'll wear you down by our capacity to suffer, and one day we will win our freedom. We will not only win freedom for ourselves, we will so appeal to your heart and conscience that we will win you in the process, and our victory will be a double victory.[3]

True peace will only come, said King, if we "finally believe in the ultimate morality of the universe, and believe that all reality hinges on moral foundations."[4]

Thus Martin Luther King made it clear that, as important as desegregation was, a truly just society rested on a moral foundation. The buses could be integrated by order of the courts, but irrational hate, fear and violence had to be overcome as well. And this is why nonviolence is so powerful: It is truth force, love force in action. The nonviolent

---

3. King, Jr., "A Christmas Sermon on Peace," in *Trumpet of Conscience*, 75.
4. King, Jr., "A Christmas Sermon on Peace," in *Trumpet of Conscience*, 76.

person who willingly suffers for the truth speaks to the heart of the opponent. The first reaction to nonviolence may well be to lash out in fury, as the British did in India to the Gandhians and as many racists in the South did to the civil rights advocates. But, at length, the British left India with enormous respect and even goodwill toward those who had been thought of as enemies. The unarmed suffering of a conquered people proved stronger than the mightiest empire of its time.

Like Gandhi, King called for a constructive program that moved from the necessary noncooperation with evil toward the next step: cooperation with good. A new society must replace the old, gaining the right to vote and developing prosperous, healthy, and progressive communities. This is a transformational approach that can "inject a new dimension of love into the veins of our civilization" that will benefit everyone. "The end is reconciliation; the end is redemption; the end is the creation of the Beloved Community."[5]

---

5. King, "Facing the Challenge of a New Age" (*Fellowship,* February 1957, 7).

The Poor People's Campaign

The need for a revolution of values led King to call for a Poor People's Campaign. This campaign, he said, was his "last, greatest dream." This would be a frontal assault on poverty, not just by Negroes, but by all the impoverished of God's children: Native Americans, Hispanics, Appalachian whites and all other poor, marginalized peoples. The crisis of America's poor, moreover, was "inseparable from an international emergency which involves the poor, the dispossessed, and the exploited of the whole world."[1]

The Poor People's Campaign was to be an attack on poverty across the nation, with the poor being brought together and trained in the discipline of nonviolence. From places all over the United States, out of local organizing and protests, the poor would begin marching toward Washington, D.C. The moral power of their cause would rally to their side all people of goodwill, the labor unions, the civil rights organizations, the religious community, intellectuals, students.

---

1. King, Jr. "Nonviolence and Social Change," in *Trumpet of Conscience*, 62.

The time had come for an economic bill of rights, and the campaign would help educate the country of its urgency and importance.

The growing rage of the dispossessed in the United States, the riots and unrest, would be addressed in a creative way by the campaign, not by violent repression but by a hopeful rechanneling of energy:

> Demonstrations have served as unifying forces in the movement; they have brought blacks and whites together in every practical situation, where philosophically they may have been arguing about black power. It's a strange thing how demonstrations tend to solve problems. The other thing is that it's little known that crime rates go down in almost every community where you have demonstrations. In Montgomery, Alabama, when we had a bus boycott, the crime rate in the Negro community went down sixty-five percent for a whole year. Anytime we've had demonstrations in a community, people have found a way to slough off their self-hatred, and they have had a channel to express their longings and a way to fight nonviolently — to get at the power structure, to know you're doing something, so you don't have to be violent to do it.[2]

The marchers would come into Washington and if the government did not respond to their appeal, they would resort to massive, nonviolent civil disobedience, placing their bodies on the line in their appeal to the American public. This would not be one or two days, but just as in the

---

2. King, Jr., "Showdown for Nonviolence," *A Testament of Hope,* 68.

other campaigns, such as Birmingham and Selma, it would last until its goal was accomplished.

The public reaction to his proposed Poor People's Campaign was extremely harsh. Widely condemned, the campaign was thought too radical, too dangerous, an unachievable fantasy. President Johnson was once again enraged at his former ally. The FBI stepped up its campaign against him, releasing scurrilous stories to many influential groups. In the heightened polarization that the Vietnam war brought to an atmosphere already poisoned by years of Cold War, many charged that King was a communist in the pay of world Communism. He was charged with sexual and financial scandals. Threats against his life increased, and a brooding sense grew in King that he did not have much time left to carry out the mission God had laid on his strong but weary shoulders. He struggled with depression and insomnia. Yet he plunged ahead with plans for the Washington campaign, sending his aides to recruit the poor from around the country and to prepare them through nonviolence training for the project. There was too much to do to stop now. The Spirit burned in him with a fierce intensity that drove him relentlessly.

King carried an underlying sense of his end drawing near, but he brought his faith to the fore in dealing with it, saying, "I cannot live in fear. I have to function. If there is one fear I have conquered, it is the fear of death."[3] He traveled around the country, meeting with Chicanos, native Americans, poor whites, holding high his dream of an integrated, dignified, nonviolent march to Washington and a three-month encampment there to bring before the nation's conscience the plight of its poor and forgotten millions. If Congress did not respond positively, the final phase of the project would

---

3. Andrew Young, "Interview," *Playboy* (July 1977), 74 cited in Oates, *Let the Trumpet Sound*, 455.

be boycotts of selected industries, supportive marches and mass civil disobedience. The aim was nothing less than a bold challenge to poverty, racism and war; his was a revolutionary call for fundamental change, born of faith in a liberating God, who calls one human family to the Beloved Community.[4]

In the hectic preparations for the Poor People's Campaign, King longed for silence, for a time to step back, to pray and reflect. And in that final spring of his life, plans were being laid for such a retreat that would take place before the beginning of the Poor People's Campaign. The black historian/activist Vincent Harding, the Quaker couple John and June Yungblut, and a few others, including the Vietnamese Zen master Thich Nhat Hanh, were in ongoing discussions with Thomas Merton, the Trappist monk at Gethsemani monastery in Kentucky, about a retreat with Dr. King. All were involved in efforts to stop the war and in such a highly charged national atmosphere, Merton wanted to be sure the retreat would be "a quiet, informal, deeply reflective session" and not be pulled into the glare of national publicity. Merton had been told by his Order to pull back from his anti-war efforts and therefore he had to move carefully and deliberately. In a letter to Harding, Merton referred to Cardinal Newman's having called for "holiness rather than peace" and added that those words took "on a new meaning in this torn-up place where everyone's idea is to obtain peace by bypassing the holiness of suffering and sacrifice and of love in which conflict is resolved."[5]

In the presidential election year of 1968 there were those who wanted King to run in a third party challenge to President Johnson. But he gave no encouragement to those

---

4. Washington, "Showdown for Nonviolence," in *Testament of Hope*, 64-72.
5. Thomas Merton, *Witness to Freedom* (New York: Farrar, Straus, Giroux, 1994), 243.

voices. He was a pastor with a prophetic calling. Throughout his tumultuous ministry, he had made every effort to be in his pulpit on Sundays and to spend time with Coretta and their four children — Yoki, Martin III, Dexter, and Bernice. Though on the world stage, he was rooted in his local community. He remained humble and approachable. On March 12, June Yungblut wrote Merton with encouraging news. She said, "Coretta King has your dates and will nail Martin down." But a few days later another letter reported that Dr. King had been urgently called to Memphis and she worried that such a tinderbox might become "Martin's Jerusalem."[6]

The fate awaiting King in Memphis would have a devastating impact on the Poor People's Campaign. The very ambitious agenda of the Campaign required the best the movement could offer and King's leadership would be sorely missed. Nonetheless the fifty thousand who gathered at the Lincoln Memorial on June 19 to conclude the Poor People's Campaign represented sectors of society — the poor of every race as well as religious, labor, and peace activists — that could carry on the building of a people's movement.[7]

---

6. Michael Mott, *The Seven Mountains of Thomas Merton* (Boston: Houghton Mifflin, 1984), 519.
7. See Young, *An Easy Burden*, 480-489.

Memphis: The Final Campaign

In the midst of preparations for the Poor People's Campaign, the sanitation workers of Memphis went on strike. King's old friend, the Rev. James Lawson, a pastor in Memphis, persuaded King to give the sanitation workers a boost in their efforts to have a union and to receive a contract giving them better wages and improved working conditions. King could not decline the call from these workers, part of the nation's poor for whom they were going to Washington. He went to Memphis to assess the situation and indicate his support. While there, he preached to a massive gathering. The situation in Memphis and the strong turnout convinced King that he should return there to assist the sanitation workers' struggle.

Meanwhile, King needed to continue his efforts for the Poor People's Campaign and also to meet with the Rabbinical Assembly of America in upstate New York. He was introduced by the scholar and civil rights activist, Rabbi Abraham Heschel, who had often marched with him and whose sixtieth birthday was being celebrated by the attending Conservative Rabbis. Introducing King he said, "The whole future of America will depend upon the impact and influence of Dr. King." He went on to say, "where in America do we hear a voice like the voice of the prophets of Israel? Martin Luther King is a sign that God has not forsaken the United States of America. God has sent him to us. His presence is the hope of America. His mission is sacred, his leadership of supreme importance to everyone of us."[1] In an extended question and answer session led by Rabbi Everett Gendler, Dr. King spoke extempore on a whole range of issues. In response to a question about anti-Semitism, he was adamant: "We have made it clear that we cannot be the victims of the notion that you deal with one evil by substituting another evil. You cannot substitute one tyranny for another, and for the black man to be struggling for justice and then turn around and be anti-Semitic is not only a very irrational course, but it is a very immoral course, and wherever we have seen anti-Semitism we have condemned it with all our might."[2]

Returning to Memphis, King led a march that had to be aborted because violence broke out by a militant group that was determined to use any means necessary to get the city's attention. But, refusing to be intimidated, King pledged to come back to lead a nonviolent march in support of the sanitation workers. Returning on April 3 and checking in at the Lorraine Motel, he very reluctantly agreed to preach to a large mass meeting that night at Mason Temple. Two thousand turned out for the meeting, even though it was a stormy night, with heavy thunder, lightning, and rain. He expressed gratitude that God had given him the chance to live in such times when there was a worldwide stirring for justice — from Johannesburg, South Africa to Nairobi,

---

1. King, Jr., meeting with the Rabbinical Assembly in New York on March 25, 1968, in Washington, *Testament of Hope*, 657.
2. King, Jr., in Washington, *Testament of Hope*, 659–668. See also Susannah Heschel, "Abraham Joshua Heschel and Martin Luther King, Jr." in *Fellowship*, Vol. 64, No. 1 (January/February, 1998), 4-6.

Kenya, to New York City, Atlanta and Memphis. He had come to Memphis to help the sanitation workers, just like the Good Samaritan had stopped to help a victim beside the road. He recounted many events of the preceding years that had led to this evening in Memphis, and then concluded by saying:

> Well, I don't know what will happen now. We've got some difficult days ahead. But it doesn't matter with me now. Because I've been to the mountaintop. And I don't mind. Like anybody, I would like to live a long life. Longevity has its place. But I'm not concerned about that now. I just want to do God's will. He's allowed me to go up to the mountain. And I've looked over. And I've seen the promised land. I may not get there with you. But I want you to know tonight, that we as a people will get to the promised land. And I'm happy tonight. I'm not worried about anything. I'm not fearing any man. Mine eyes have seen the glory of the coming of the Lord.[3]

Looking back on this soul-stirring valedictory sermon, Andrew Young reflects that "in a rare moment born of inner turmoil, inner questioning, and self-doubt during those days in which his leadership was sorely questioned and challenged, [King] may have seen as we could not, that his time was passing, that he had done all he could on earth."[4] Twelve years earlier, as he prayed at the kitchen table in his Montgomery parsonage, he had struggled with awesome demands placed on him as he had taken up the leadership of the bus boycott. Not only his life but the lives of his family had been repeatedly threatened. Walking through

---

3. Washington, "I See the Promised Land," in *Testament of Hope*, 279-286.
4. Young, *An Easy Burden*, 463.

the valley of the shadow of death, he had placed himself in the hands of God and had found reassurance in an inner voice that said, "Stand up for righteousness, stand up for truth; and God will be at your side forever." And now in Memphis he faced another transforming moment in his faith journey. Not only had violent elements disrupted the first Memphis march supporting the sanitation worker's strike, but there was widespread and harsh criticism of the Poor People's Campaign as well as the continuing disparagement of his anti-war leadership and his unwavering commitment to nonviolence. The admonition of Jesus had undergirded him: "Blessed are you when men shall revile you and persecute you and say all manner of evil against you falsely for my sake. Rejoice and be exceedingly glad, for so persecuted they the prophets which were before you."

As he delivered what was to be his final sermon, he was at peace with God, whatever the future might have had in store. In the darkness of the night, he had seen the stars and they beckoned him on into the unknown as he sought to do God's will.

Stirred by the great response of the service that night, King took heart, returning to the motel in good spirits. The next day, April 4, he and his staff prepared to go to Rev. Samuel Kyles' home for dinner. Before they left, King stepped out on the balcony beside his room and chatted with friends below. He asked Jesse Jackson to make sure his favorite song, "Precious Lord, Take My Hand" would be played at the evening meeting. A few moments later he was felled by an assassin's bullet that tore into the right side of his chin. The shot was fatal, despite the desperate efforts of Ralph Abernathy, Andrew Young, and others to stop the massive bleeding. By the time he reached the hospital it was too late. The prophet of nonviolence was dead.[5]

---

5. Abernathy, *And the Walls Came Tumbling Down*, 440.

Violence broke out across the country, but after three days it began to subside. Those who called for rioting and rebellion in the wake of the assassination did not carry the day. Saner voices prevailed such as James Farmer who said, "The only fitting memorial to this martyred leader is a monumental commitment now — not a day later — to eliminate racism. Dr. King hated bloodshed. His own blood must not now trigger more bloodshed."[6]

---

6. Abernathy, *And the Walls Came Tumbling Down*, 451.

The World Grieves
Its Fallen Prophet

President Johnson proclaimed Sunday, April 7, a day of national mourning. Flags across the country flew at half mast. On April 8, Coretta King and her three oldest children, joined by Ralph Abernathy, led a silent march of 19,000 through the streets of Memphis. The next week the strike ended when the city recognized the union and the demands of the strikers.

On April 9, Martin Luther King, Jr., was buried in Atlanta. As many as one hundred thousand mourners gathered outside a packed Ebenezer Baptist Church. Joining the King family, civil rights leaders, and black dignitaries such as Harry Belafonte, Mahalia Jackson, Thurgood Marshall, Sammy Davis, Jr., Floyd Patterson, and Diana Ross, were Jacqueline Kennedy, Vice President Hubert Humphrey, Nelson Rockefeller, Richard Nixon, Attorney General Ramsey Clark, and Ethel and Robert Kennedy (who would be murdered only two months later). Dr. King was carried from the church in a wooden wagon drawn by two mules, a vivid symbol of his last dream for the world's poor, a reminder that he was murdered while defending the rights of exploited sanitation workers.

The funeral procession went from Ebenezer to the historic quadrangle at Morehouse College where King had first read Henry David Thoreau, one of the great advocates of nonviolence. There in the service held in the quadrangle Benjamin Mays paid tribute to the fallen martyr:

> We have assembled here from every section of this great nation and from other parts of the world to give thanks to God that He gave to America, at this moment in history, Martin Luther King, Jr. Truly God is no respecter of persons. How strange! God called the grandson of a slave . . . and said to him: Martin Luther, speak to America about war and peace; about social justice and racial discrimination; about its obligation to the poor; and about nonviolence as a way of perfecting social change in a world of brutality and war.[1]

Rabbi Heschel read from the Psalms and Rev. Abernathy preached from the Joseph story in Genesis where the brothers conspire against Joseph.

Dr. King was buried in the South View Cemetery near his grandparents. Later, his crypt found its final resting place at the Martin Luther King, Jr., Center for Nonviolent Social Change on Auburn Street near the Ebenezer Baptist Church, which King had served so faithfully, as had his father and grandfather before him. On the marble crypt are inscribed the words of the spiritual King often quoted in his speeches and sermons, "Free at Last, Free at Last, Thank God Almighty, I'm Free at Last!"

---

1. Oates, *Let the Trumpet Sound*, 497.

To this day disturbing, unanswered questions remain about the assassination of King. Although James Earl Ray was quickly charged and sent to prison, much of the evidence was not examined nor a thorough investigation made. Since 1968, the Rev. James Lawson, Attorney William Pepper, and others have continued efforts to examine all the evidence and discover whether powerful forces may have planned and carried out the assassination. Although public opinion is weighted against these efforts, wanting to move beyond this painful event, others feel we owe it to King, and to ourselves, to seek the truth, wherever it leads, for truth has a cleansing and healing power.[2]

In the year before James Earl Ray died in prison in 1998, the King family for the first time spoke publicly of their belief that Ray did not kill Dr. King. Mrs. King appealed to President Clinton to set up a Truth and Reconciliation Commission (patterned after South Africa's Commission) to open up the assassination to a thorough and careful examination with the intention of discovering who killed King and under whose direction. Without such an investigation the truth remains in doubt, the alleged conspirators unknown, the democratic process poisoned.

Surely this we know: Martin Luther King, Jr. was a person touched by the spirit of God, calling the whole human family to become the Beloved Community where peace and justice reign. In 1977, President Carter posthumously awarded King the Presidential Medal of Freedom, calling him "the conscience of his generation." Furthermore he said,

> He made our nation stronger because he made
> it better. Honored by kings, he continued to his

---

2. See, for example, William Pepper, *Orders to Kill*; Andrew Young, *An Easy Burden*, 470-73; and "The Truth Behind the Murder of Martin Luther King, Jr.," interview of James Lawson by Richard Deats, *Fellowship* (March/April 1996): 4-7.

last days to strive for a world where the poorest and the humblest among us could enjoy the fulfillment of the promises of our founding fathers.

His life informed us, his dreams sustain us yet.[3]

---

3. President Jimmy Carter in epigraph of Washington, *Testament of Hope*.

Epilogue

At the place where Martin Luther King, Jr. was gunned down on the balcony of the Lorraine Motel in Memphis, Tennessee, there is a simple plaque with an inscription from the story in the Bible where Joseph's brothers plot to get rid of him:

> Here comes the dreamer. Come now, let us kill him . . . and we shall see what will become of his dreams. (Gn 37:19-20)

Dr. King was killed at the age of thirty-nine, his ministry cut short after only a few brief years. Those who cheered when he died—and there were many—thought he had finally been silenced. But the dream of the promised land has been placed in the human heart for all eternity, and that dream cannot be killed. As Vincent Harding, African-American professor of religion and social transformation at Iliff School of Theology, has written, "King lives . . . we saw him facing the tanks in Tiananmen Square, dancing on the crumbling wall of

Berlin, singing in Prague, alive in the glistening eyes of Nelson Mandela . . . he lives within us, right here, wherever his message is expanded and carried out in our daily lives, wherever his unfinished battles are taken up by our hands."[1]

As King approached that final day in Memphis, the fire of God's light and love and life burned ever more insistently in him. He reached out to embrace the whole earth with "the fierce urgency of Now." He had risen to prominence as a civil rights leader of African-Americans. At the end of his life his final passion was for all of God's poor — black and white, brown, yellow, and red. And he was looking beyond his own country, envisioning nonviolent liberation throughout the world. From the mountaintop of faith he had a foretaste of that final reconciliation God is calling us to. Our hearts tremble as we too seek to follow that Light, wherever it leads, whatever the cost.

We ponder the mystery of God's luminous presence that shone so brightly in this disciple of Jesus. And we are hushed in awe and gratitude for such a life. In one of Shakespeare's plays[2] are words that could be said about Martin Luther King, Jr., spirit-led prophet:

> Take him and cut him out in little stars,
> And he will make the face of heaven so fine
> That all the world will be in love with night.

Black Knight of the nonviolent God, your stars still burn brightly in the night and our way is illumined.

---

1. Vincent Harding, *Martin Luther King: The Inconvenient Hero* (Maryknoll, NY: Orbis Books, 1996), 136.
2. *Romeo and Juliet* III, ii, 21.

Chronology

1929   (January 15) Martin Luther King, Jr., born in Atlanta, the son of Alberta Christine Williams King and Martin Luther King, Sr.

1944   King enters Morehouse College in Atlanta, an early admissions freshman.

1948   (February 25) King is ordained to the Baptist ministry.
        (June) King graduates from Morehouse College with a Bachelor of Arts degree and a major in sociology.

        (September) King enters Crozer Theological Seminary in Chester, Pennsylvania.

1951   (June) King graduates from Crozer Seminary with a Bachelor of Divinity degree.
        (September 13) King enters the doctoral program at Boston University School of Theology.

1953   (June 18) King is married to Coretta Scott by Martin Luther King, Sr., at the Scott home near Marion, Alabama.

1954   (May 17) The U.S. Supreme Court declares in Brown
        vs. Board of Education of Topeka that segregation in
        public schools is unconstitutional.

        (September 1) King becomes pastor of Dexter Avenue
        Baptist Church in Montgomery, Alabama.

1955   (June 5) King is awarded his Ph.D. in Systematic
        Theology from Boston University. His dissertation
        topic is "A Comparison of the Conceptions of God in
        the Thinking of Paul Tillich and Henry Nelson
        Weiman."

        (November 17) The first child of Martin and Coretta,
        Yolanda Denise, is born.

        (December 1) Rosa Parks is arrested in Montgomery for
        refusing to move to the back of the bus. Her arrest leads
        to the founding of the Montgomery Improvement
        Association, with King elected as its president. The MIA
        calls for a boycott of city buses, which lasts from
        December 5, 1955 to December 21, 1956.

1956   (January 30) The Kings' home is bombed. A few days
        earlier, on Jan. 26, King is arrested for the first time.

        (February 21) King is arrested for going 30 mph in a 25
        mph zone.

1957   (January 10-11). The Southern Christian Leadership
        Conference is founded and Dr. King becomes its first
        president.

        (October 23) Martin Luther III is born to the Kings.

1958   (September 20) King is stabbed in New York City while
        autographing copies of his first book, *Stride Toward
        Freedom*, which had just been released.

1959   (February 2–March 10) Coretta and Martin King are
        Prime Minister Nehru's guests in India where they
        study Mahatma Gandhi's life and thought.

1960   King becomes co-pastor, with his father, of Ebenezer
        Baptist Church in Atlanta. Sit-ins spread across the
        United States. John Kennedy is elected president.

1961   (January 30) Dexter, the third King child, is born.
        (November 1961–August 1962) The Albany Movement.
        Freedom Rides test segregated interstate travel.

1962   Rioting follows the court ordered enrollment of James
        Meredith at the University of Mississippi. President
        Kennedy federalizes Mississippi troops on September
        29 to restore order.

1963   (March 28) Bernice, the King's fourth child, is born.
        (April 3–May 10) Birmingham Campaign to
        desegregate public accommodations. While in jail, King
        writes "Letter from a Birmingham Jail."

        (June) Dr. King's *Strength to Love* is published.

        (June 12) Medgar Evers, field director for the NAACP in
        Jackson, Mississippi is murdered in front of his home.

        (August 28) King delivers "I Have a Dream" speech at
        the Lincoln Memorial at the conclusion of the March on
        Washington D.C. for Civil Rights.

        (September 15) Sixteenth Avenue Baptist Church in
        Birmingham is bombed, resulting in the death of four
        girls. King preaches the eulogy.

        (November 22) President Kennedy is assassinated in
        Dallas motorcade.

1964   (March–June) St. Augustine March. Dr. King's book,
        Why We Can't Wait, is published. Mississippi Freedom
        Summer. Civil rights workers James Chaney, Andrew
        Goodman, and Michael Schwerner murdered.
        (September 18) Dr. King has an audience with Pope
        Paul VI at the Vatican.

        (December 10) King awarded Nobel Peace Prize.

1965   (January–March) Selma Campaign to secure voting
        rights culminates with march to Montgomery.
        (February 21) Malcolm X assassinated.

        (August 6) President Johnson signs Voting Rights Act.

1966   Chicago Campaign to challenge "the violence of poverty." King family moves into slum flat in Chicago. (May) King becomes co-chairman of Clergy & Laity Concerned about Vietnam.

        (June 6) James Meredith is shot on his "March Against Fear" from Memphis, Tennessee to Jackson, Mississippi.

1967   King increasingly addresses the violence of the Vietnam war and on April 4 delivers a major address on the war at Riverside Church in New York City. King writes his last book, *Where Do We Go from Here: Chaos or Community?*

1968   King calls for a Poor People's Campaign. On March 31 he preaches his last Sunday sermon, "Remaining Awake Through a Great Revolution," at the National Cathedral (Episcopal) in Washington, D.C.
        (April 3) In Memphis to support the sanitation workers' strike, King preaches final sermon, "I See the Promised Land," at Mason Temple.

        (April 4) King is assassinated on the balcony of the Lorraine Motel in Memphis.

        (April 9) King is buried in Atlanta.

        (June 5) Robert Kennedy is assassinated in California after winning that state's primary in his presidential campaign.

1983   (November 2) President Reagan signs the bill establishing the birthday of Martin Luther King, Jr., as an American national holiday. It is observed on the third Monday of January. The first official observance is in 1986.

Sources

The selections from Martin Luther King's writings found in this book are used with permission. I would like to thank the contributing publishers for their support in this biography.

The Papers of Martin Luther King, Jr. Vol. I, *Called to Serve (January 1929–June 1951)*. Edited by Clayborne Carson. Berkeley: University of California Press, 1992.

Stride Toward Freedom. New York: Harper & Brothers Publishers, 1958.

Where Do We Go from Here: Chaos or Community? New York: Harper & Row, 1968.

The Testament of Hope: The Essential Writings and Speeches of Martin Luther King, Jr. Edited by James M. Washington. San Francisco: Harper Collins, 1991.

"Walk for Freedom," *Fellowship* 22 (May 1956).

Why We Can't Wait. New York: Mentor Penguin Books, 1963.

Strength to Love. Philadelphia: Fortress Press, 1983.

The Trumpet of Conscience. San Francisco: Harper & Row, 1987.

"Facing the Challenge of a New Age," *Fellowship* 23 (February 1957).

Selected Bibliography

The Works of Martin Luther King, Jr.

A Knock at Midnight. Edited by Clayborne Carson and Peter Holloran. New York: Warner Books, Inc. 1998.

The Measure of a Man. Philadelphia: Fortress Press, 1959.

The Papers of Martin Luther King, Jr. Edited by Clayborn Carson. Berkeley: University of California Press, 1992. Vol. 1 *Called to Serve* (January 1929–June 1951). Vol. 2 *Rediscovering Precious Values* (July 1951–November 1955).

Strength to Love. Philadelphia: Fortress Press, 1983.

Stride Toward Freedom. New York: Harper & Brothers Publishers, 1958.

The Testament of Hope: The Essential Writings and Speeches of Martin Luther King, Jr. Edited by James M. Washington. San Francisco: Harper Collins, 1991.

The Trumpet of Conscience. San Francisco: Harper & Row, 1987.

Where Do We Go From Here: Chaos or Community? New York: Harper & Row, 1968.

Why We Can't Wait. New York: Mentor (Penguin Books), 1963.

Works About Martin Luther King, Jr.

Branch, Taylor P. *The Parting of the Waters: America During the King Years, 1954-63*. New York: Simon & Schuster, 1988.

――――――. *Pillar of Fire. America in the King Years, 1963-65*. New York: Simon & Schuster, 1998.

Cone, James H. *Martin and Malcolm in America*. Maryknoll, New York: Orbis Books, 1986.

Douglass, James W. *Compassion and the Unspeakable in the Murders of Martin, Malcolm, JFK, RFK*. Lanett, AL: Project Hope, 1998.

Garrow, David. *Bearing the Cross: Martin Luther King, Jr. and the Southern Christian Leadership Conference*. New York: William Morrow, 1986.

Harding, Vincent. *Martin Luther King: The Inconvenient Hero*. Maryknoll, New York: Orbis Books, 1996.

King, Coretta Scott. *My Life with Martin Luther King, Jr.* New York: Holt, Rinehart, and Winston, 1969.

King, Martin Luther, Sr. with Clayton Riley. *Daddy King: An Autobiography*. New York: William Morrow, 1980.

Lewis, John. *Walking with the Wind. A Memoir of the Movement*. New York: Simon & Schuster, 1998.

Miller, William Robert. *Martin Luther King, Jr. His Life, Martyrdom and Meaning for the Word*. New York: Weybright and Talley, 1968.

Oates, Stephen B. *Let the Trumpet Sound: The Life of Martin Luther King, Jr.* New York: Harper & Row Publishers, 1982.

Pepper, William F. *Orders to Kill: The Truth Behind the Murder of Martin Luther King*. New York: Carroll & Graf Publishers, Inc., 1995.

Young, Andrew. *An Easy Burden. The Civil Rights Movement and the Transformation of America*. New York: Harper Collins Publishers, 1996.

Acknowledgments

I am grateful to the many persons who have helped make this biography possible. First of all I am indebted to Coretta Scott King who encouraged me along the way, who carefully read the manuscript and offered many helpful insights, corrections and suggestions, and, finally, wrote a most gracious Foreword.

Dexter King, president of the Martin Luther King, Jr. Center for Nonviolent Social Change, took a personal interest in the book for which I am very grateful. I am also indebted to Lili Baxter, Steve Klein and Lynn Cothren who were unfailingly helpful with my many requests and inquiries. Dorothy Cotton offered advice and encouragement, as did James Lawson, Lou Ann Ha'aheo Guanson, Jo Becker, John Dear, Gerald H. Anderson, Walter Wink, Lee Riffaterre and Mairead Corrigan Maguire. Michelle Rubin of Writers' House was most helpful.

New City Press, which first conceived this project, has been completely supportive from the very beginning. It has been a pleasure to work with them, especially with their editor, Patrick Markey, who never stopped working to bring this book to fruition. Any errors or omissions, however, are due solely to me.

Finally I wish to thank my wife, Jan, who always knew that *Martin Luther King, Jr. Spirit-Led Prophet* would be published.

Index

155